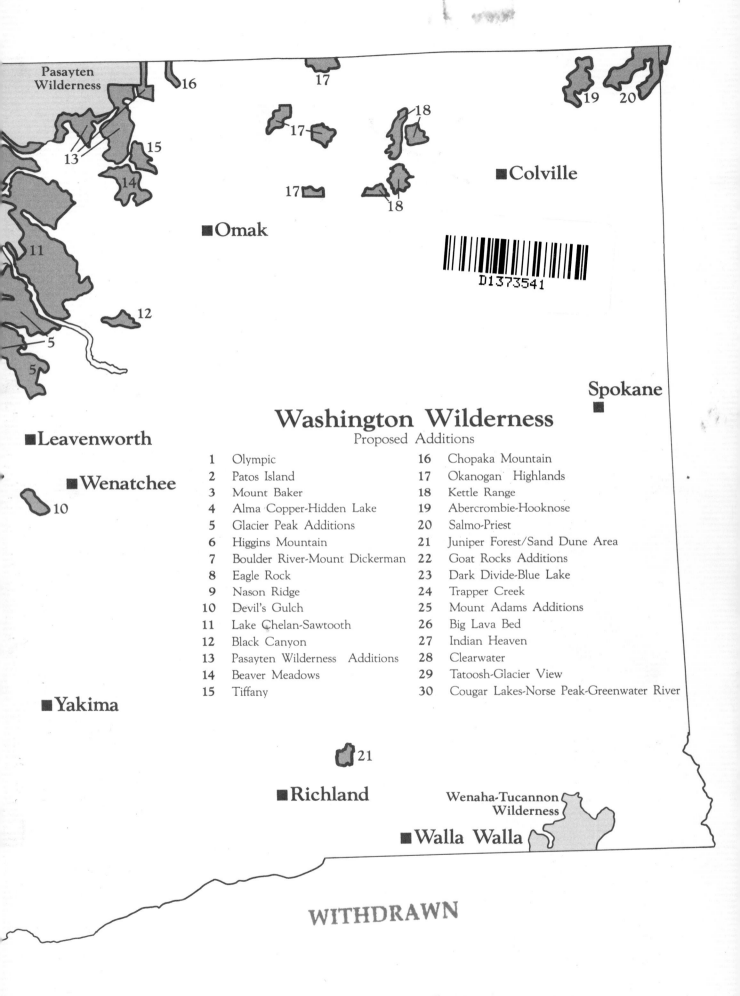

Pasayten
Wilderness

16

17

17

18

18

■Colville

17

■Omak

15

13

14

11

12

5

5

Spokane
■

■Leavenworth

Washington Wilderness
Proposed Additions

■Wenatchee

10

1	Olympic	16	Chopaka Mountain
2	Patos Island	17	Okanogan Highlands
3	Mount Baker	18	Kettle Range
4	Alma Copper-Hidden Lake	19	Abercrombie-Hooknose
5	Glacier Peak Additions	20	Salmo-Priest
6	Higgins Mountain	21	Juniper Forest/Sand Dune Area
7	Boulder River-Mount Dickerman	22	Goat Rocks Additions
8	Eagle Rock	23	Dark Divide-Blue Lake
9	Nason Ridge	24	Trapper Creek
10	Devil's Gulch	25	Mount Adams Additions
11	Lake Chelan-Sawtooth	26	Big Lava Bed
12	Black Canyon	27	Indian Heaven
13	Pasayten Wilderness Additions	28	Clearwater
14	Beaver Meadows	29	Tatoosh-Glacier View
15	Tiffany	30	Cougar Lakes-Norse Peak-Greenwater River

■Yakima

21

■Richland

Wenaha-Tucannon
Wilderness

■Walla Walla

WITHDRAWN

Dedicated to the 88th Congress,
which acted with both wisdom and foresight
when it passed the Wilderness Act of 1964.
In doing so it acknowledged
a need for places where...

...the earth and its community of life are untrammeled by man,
where man himself is a visitor who does not remain.

Washington Wilderness

THE UNFINISHED WORK

HARVEY MANNING

PHOTOGRAPHY BY PAT O'HARA

THE MOUNTAINEERS · SEATTLE

©1984 by Harvey Manning, Pat O'Hara,
and Richard Rutz

Published by The Mountaineers
300 Third Avenue West, Seattle, Washington 98119

Published simultaneously in Canada by
Douglas & McIntyre, Ltd.
1615 Venables Street, Vancouver,
British Columbia V5L 2H1

Designed by Dianne Hofbeck
Edited by Deborah Easter
Maps by Katy Huston

Photo of mountain caribou on page 78
courtesy of Parks Canada.

Typesetting by Scarlet Letters Ltd., Seattle.

Color separations, printing, and binding by
Dai Nippon Printing Co., Ltd., Tokyo, Japan

Library of Congress Cataloging in
Publication Data

Manning, Harvey.
    Washington wilderness.

    Includes index.
    1. Wilderness areas—Washington (State)
2. National parks and reserves—Washington
(State) I. O'Hara, Pat, 1947-   . II. Title.
QH76.5.W2M36 1984   333.95'16'09797   83-13497
ISBN 0-89886-006-7

Above - Droplets on grass, Hoh Rain Forest

Overleaf - Gray Wolf River, Olympic Forest

CONTENTS

*The Mountaineers gratefully acknowledges
the generous memorial contribution toward the
publication of this book from the family of
Marjorie Muffly Reynolds and
Rodney Floyd Reynolds,
longtime Mountaineers who loved life
and cherished nature.*

Mount Baker

*To preserve, by protective legislation or otherwise,
the natural beauty of Northwest America*
— from The Mountaineers Articles of Incorporation

PUBLISHER'S STATEMENT

The *Mountaineers* club was organized in 1906 to climb mountains; however, the purposes and goals of the club encompass much more than that. The Mountaineers are people who love the mountains, valleys and forests, rivers and lakes, flowers and wildlife. They seek to see and enjoy these beauties of nature, now and in the future. The people of the Northwest are indeed fortunate that much natural beauty still remains, that the appreciation for nature and its creations has developed while there is still time to save them. To the preservation of this heritage, The Mountaineers is dedicated. As Dr. Henry Landes, first president of The Mountaineers, wrote in 1907: we seek "to render a public service in the battle to preserve our natural scenery from wanton destruction."

The key feature of wilderness areas is their naturalness, their relative freedom from significant alterations by humans. Congress, in passing the Wilderness Act in 1964, established the National Wilderness Preservation System "to secure for the American people of present and future generations the benefits of an enduring resource of wilderness." The Mountaineers fully supports this policy: since the founding of the club, The Mountaineers has been involved in most of the great conservation and preservation battles in the Northwest, and has played a leading role in securing and protecting the national parks and wildernesses in Washington State.

ACKNOWLEDGMENTS

The concept of a book celebrating Washington's wilderness originated several years ago within The Mountaineers and was further refined by the work and ideas of many persons both within and outside of the club. The book itself became a reality through the efforts of a group of dedicated volunteers. It is not possible to name every individual and organization that contributed to the shaping of the project, but special acknowledgment is due at least to the following: to Charlie Raines, for allowing the photographer to draw upon his exhaustive wilderness knowledge; to the club's Conservation Division for its inspiration and perseverance; and to members of the ad hoc committee formed from the division and the Editorial Review Committee expressly for the purpose of guiding the book through to its completion: Jo Roberts, chair; Dick Barden, Marc Bardsley, Richard Rutz, Norm Winn, Polly Dyer and Connie Pious.

FOREWORD

Life is built on a framework of memories. Each moment we add to our storehouse—some never to be recalled, some retrieved regularly, and some brought back vividly by the trigger of voice, aroma, sight, or sound.

In today's technological, fast-paced, and sometimes transitory society, we are overwhelmed by electronic messages that create a jumble of chaotic and unfinished memories. We increasingly long for the simple, traditional, and natural experiences that will help steady us in an uncertain world.

A generation of wilderness expeditions return to me again and again through full-color memories as sharp and clear as the original experiences. Each can be savored as sustenance and continuity when dismay over current events overwhelms me.

I remember sitting with my eight-year-old son on a mountain hillside watching, hushed, as a bear quietly browsed through the meadow, oblivious to us. As quiet enveloped us, senses sharpened and we gradually noticed the slow hum of nearby honeybees, the haunting whistle of a far-off varied thrush, and the deep rumble of the river hidden in the canyon far below. Never had I felt closer to my son.

I remember drinking from a hundred mountain streams. Water, numbingly cold and clear, with a faint flavor of the hillside meadow, a restorative better than fine vintage wine.

I remember plodding slowly toward Asgaard Pass and hearing the cry of wonder as our boys clambered over the top and stood in awe of the Martian landscape before them. Slabs and pinnacles of ice gray rock plastered with snow teasingly visible and then gone, swept away in the turbulence of an infinite fog. Tiny flowers peeked from every crevice, thumbing their blossomed noses at the attacking wind. A shaft of sunlight pierced the gloom and silently, magically, the fog curtain rolled back. The carpet of moss caressing the Enchantment Lakes appeared and what was alien and harsh suddenly turned benign. Who could forget?

I remember lying naked on a smooth rock engulfed by the warmth of the sun from stone and sky. The brilliant blue above challenged the deeper tones of the nearby mountain lake. The tiny basin, ringed on all sides by mountain peaks and summer snowfields glittered with the explosion of a wildflower rainbow. An enormous sense of peace and well-being enveloped me in this moment divorced from all impediments of our modern society.

I remember lying in a sleeping bag on a mountain ridge glorying over stars never seen from the city and marveling over the frequent paths of artificial satellites, tracking across the sky. The unknown depths of the universe sent shivers down my spine.

What a joy to draw from this inexhaustible and undiminished store of memories.

As governor I was often challenged about wilderness. Why set aside so much for so few? How much is enough? Why not a road access so everyone can enjoy it? These are challenging and not always easy questions. Pressures for wilderness use are already overwhelming us. Rationing of visits already occurs. The two thousand cardholders of Recreational Equipment Cooperative in my youth have grown to more than a million today.

When there is doubt, I hope we will always preserve wilderness. If ultimately we have too much, uses can be changed, but wilderness destroyed cannot be regained.

We must leave to our twenty-first century children two important legacies: all of the knowledge we possess on which they will build in ways we cannot yet foresee, and wilderness preserves or windows to the past where they can stand and say, "This is how it was before man touched the earth."

— *Senator Daniel J. Evans*
Governor of Washington 1965-1977
President of Evergreen State College 1977-1983

Larch trees and Little Annapurna, Alpine Lakes Wilderness

Autumn Reflection, Wenatchee Forest

Aspen trees, Wenaha-Tucannon Wilderness

Overleaf - *Goat Peak and Mount Shuksan from the Mount Baker Area (proposal)*

Stream in the Lake Chelan-Sawtooth Area

Sand dune in the Juniper Forest

PART I

The Last Century/
The Last Decade

Wilderness is not a luxury—it is essential to all civilized people, even to those who never go there. As the highland creeks have been destabilized by logging and their floods have flushed billions of tons of soil down to the sea, and the water supplies of the cities have grown more polluted, and as fish have vanished from formerly teeming streams, and as wild animals and birds have suffered catastrophes the more tragic because unnoticed, and as the chemical and physical manipulation of enormous acreages has threatened the size and diversity of Earth's gene pool, it has become evident that wilderness is not the business merely of hikers seeking refuge but of the entire community of life.

The federal census of 1870, the second since there had been a Seattle, counted 1,107 people in the village. Several years earlier the U.S. North West Boundary Survey, assigned to collaborate with a British counterpart in marking the international border, published its map of Washington Territory. The sole major land-travel route shown west of the Cascades is the Military Road from Olympia and Fort Nisqually north to Fort Whatcom, along the way passing through Steilacoom, Seattle, Snohomish City, Sehome ("coal mines"), and Whatcom—only these settlements and no others.

The map shows a few verified and "reported" trails. Otherwise it is a territory dominated by blank space (the Olympics); "unexplored" (Mount Baker); "covered with pine forest" (Mount Adams and Mount St. Helens); and "sand barrens" (today known as the Juniper Forest). There obviously is a deep-felt need for a strong military presence.

The 1890 census counted 42,837 Seattle residents, nearly that many in Tacoma, and sizable populations in rows of new towns and cities along saltwater shores, rivers, proliferating wagon roads, and burgeoning railroads. The Superintendent of the Census announced in his report that during the prior decade the American frontier had ceased to be the unbroken line it had been for centuries and henceforth would not be officially noted. Citizens of the new (1889) Washington State could nod with satisfaction at the superintendent's observation. In twenty years they had progressed from frontier to civilization, from rounding up Indians to battling Eastern bankers and railroad tycoons.

Since Jamestown and Plymouth Rock the American policy on land had been to get it away from Spaniards or Indians or whomever and then to get it out of the public domain into the private. In 1846 Great Britain and the United States carved up the Northwest between them; in 1854-55 the Indians were assigned their share in the treaties that caused the Indian Wars. The Donation Land Law of 1850, Homestead Act of 1862, Mining Laws of 1872, Timber Culture Act of 1873, and Timber and Stone Act of 1878 expedited private preemption of public land. Land also could be directly purchased (the transactions often oiled by bribes) from the Federal Land Offices; from the Northern Pacific Railroad, which in 1864 had been given forty million acres by a bribed Congress (as historians have abundantly documented), including nearly a quarter of what was to become the state of Washington; or after 1889 from the state, which was granted lands for support of schools and other institutions, and whose officials so routinely augmented their pay with bribes that it was not thought worthy of comment except when they angered colleagues by taking more than their share.

During the twenty years in which Seattle's population increased nearly fortyfold, the volume of land transactions in Washington—as throughout the West—kept pace. Observers began to understand that the American earth was not, as previously assumed, infinite. They also noted that Western lumbermen frequently did not even bother to bribe officials but simply cut the trees. Investigators during the administration of President Ulysses S. Grant (1869-77) estimated that forty million dollars worth of timber had been stolen from the public lands of Washington Territory.

Overleaf - *Naches River Valley, Cougar Lakes Area, Mt. Adams in distance*

In 1891 Congress belatedly and half-heartedly reacted by passing the Forest Reserve Act, which reserved lands from preemption but made no provision for their management or protection. In 1893 President Grover Cleveland used the act's authority to give Washington its first area secured from private enterprise, the Pacific Forest Reserve centered on Mount Rainier.

The legislation was so flawed that the Secretary of the Interior, at the urging of the American Forestry Association, asked the National Academy of Science to sponsor a study. In the summer of 1896 the seven-member National Forest Commission, including Gifford Pinchot, a young man of wealth who had studied in Europe and made himself "America's first professional forester," and John Muir, in his late fifties and long since a legend, toured the West. The commission recommended the creation of thirteen new forest reserves and the addition of two new national parks to the existing four—Grand Canyon and Mount Rainier.

On February 22, 1897, with ten days left in his administration, President Cleveland received a summary of the commission's report and proceeded to proclaim the reserves, three of them in Washington—Olympic, Washington (in the North Cascades), and Mount Rainier (an enlargement of the Pacific Forest Reserve). The same year Congress passed the Forestry Act, subsequently hailed as the "Magna Carta of American forestry" for declaring: "No public forest reservation shall be established except to improve and protect the forest within the reservation, or for the purpose of securing favorable conditions of waterflow, and to furnish a continuous supply of timber for the use and necessities of citizens of the United States." This "Magna Carta" repaired some defects of the 1891 act by an explicit declaration of purpose; by omission it implied those matters that "American forestry" would *not* concern itself with.

The subsequent story of the reserves is that of Gifford Pinchot. In 1898 he gained a power base as Chief of the Division of Forestry in the Department of Agriculture. In 1905 Congress passed the Transfer Act, moving the reserves from the Department of Interior to Pinchot's agency, soon renamed the U.S. Forest Service,

*Fog-shrouded conifers,
Clearwater River*

with Pinchot the Chief Forester. Two years later the reserves were renamed "national forests."

The national forests grew by leaps and bounds as Pinchot's field agents sped through the West, racing the lumbermen's timber cruisers and hired preemptors (individuals who would preempt land to sell the rights to a timber company and then move on to their next preemption). The federal agents marked boundaries for new forests, and Pinchot's devoted friend, President Theodore Roosevelt, signed proclamations. In 1907 Congress recoiled in horror and revoked the presidential right to proclaim national forests in certain states, Washington among them. In the final days before the revocation took effect, Roosevelt signed thirty-three proclamations, bringing the national forests of the West to essentially the bounds they have today in the old forty-eight states.

In later years there would be debates about what Pinchot meant in his Letter of Instructions (signed by the Secretary of Agriculture, addressed to the Chief Forester, but written by Pinchot): "Where conflicting interests must be reconciled the question will always be decided from the standpoint of the greatest good of the greatest number in the long run." At the time of writing in 1905, however, Pinchot was clearly understood as intending the deathblow to cut-and-run logging (and eat-and-run grazing) on all federal lands. Had Congress granted him the regulatory power he sought, the Forest Service would have done the same on state and private lands that were deemed to have national importance. There would not be, as now, at least half a dozen separate, uncoordinated, and in many respects conflicting "forest policies" in the state of Washington.

Pinchot's creed was the wise use of natural resources to ensure a steady supply for future generations. To define his philosophy he adapted a concept from the forest conservancies set aside by the British in India and made "conservation" his battle cry. In a sense the true end of the frontier was not 1890 but 1905.

In another sense, though, Pinchot's reforms were designed to perpetuate the frontier—under government supervision. Himself an admirer of natural beauty, he could let the glaciers and meadows of Mount Rainier be—but not the forests. Above all he was a nine-

teenth-century utilitarian and in his mold he created the U.S. Forest Service.

•   •   •

A few atypical frontier dwellers did not march solely to the clink of coins. In Montana a group introduced to the wonders of Yellowstone did not rush to file preemption claims but instead sought the ear of Congress, which in 1872 established Yellowstone National Park— the nation's first—as a "public park or pleasuring ground for the benefit and enjoyment of the people." John Muir and friends publicized the splendors of the Sierra of California and in 1890 Congress created Yosemite, Sequoia, and General Grant (later part of Kings Canyon) National Parks. In 1899 Washington became the third state to have a national park, Mount Rainier.

The wildlands, through the ages considered the habitat of the Enemy of Mankind, began to be admired, even loved, most passionately by people who did not have to live in them and temporarily abandoned the comforts of cities to revel in hardships their ancestors had labored millennia to avoid. In 1892 the Sierra Club was formed in California, with John Muir as the first president, "To explore, enjoy, and preserve...forests, waters, wildlife, and wilderness..." In 1894 The Mazamas (the Spanish name for mountain goats) was founded in Oregon, followed in 1906 by The Mountaineers in Washington, to "preserve by the encouragement of protective legislation or otherwise the natural beauty of Northwest America."

Stimulated by the newspaper and magazine reports of the expeditions of these clubs and other explorers, the national park concept captured America. In 1892 the townsfolk of Chelan proposed a park to halt the slaughter of mountain goats and bears along Lake Chelan. In 1906 The Mazamas proposed a park for the same area, as did the Wenatchee Chamber of Commerce in 1919. From 1908 to 1919 nine bills were introduced in Congress to establish a Mount Baker National Park, promoted by the Mount Baker Club of Bellingham, and from 1919 to 1921 three bills were introduced, supported by the Spokane and Yakima chambers of commerce, to create a Yakima National Park to duly honor Mount Adams and environs.

These were late entries. In the summer of 1890, Lieutenant Joseph P. O'Neil of the U.S. Army and Judge James Wickersham had agreed while on an expedition across the Olympics that the range belonged in a park. Wickersham subsequently drew up a proposal. It was too soon then, and still not time in 1907, when The Mountaineers held its first summer outing —to Mount Olympus—and succeeded in getting a park bill introduced, but not passed, in Congress. However, in 1906 Congress had passed the Antiquities Act empowering the president to establish national monuments to protect scenes of historic or scientific interest, and in 1909 President Roosevelt, two days before leaving office, proclaimed—at the instigation of members of The Mountaineers—Mount Olympus National Monument, the state's second area, after Rainier, preserved from exploitation.

In 1916 the National Park Act gave the preservation movement its own agency, the National Park Service, in the Department of

Gray Wolf Ridge,
Olympic National Park

Cloud-capped Mount Rainier

15

Interior, and its own statement of purpose: "To conserve the scenery and the natural and historic objects and the wildlife therein [in the national parks] and to provide for the enjoyment of the same in such manner and by such means as will leave them unimpaired for the enjoyment of future generations."

The difference between the U.S. Forest Service and the National Park Service was the difference between Gifford Pinchot, who created the former, and John Muir, who was an important force in the creation of the latter. Muir fully agreed with Pinchot on the necessity of the wise use of natural resources. However, he felt the wisest use of *some* resources was *preservation*, quite another thing than *conservation*. In contrast to Pinchot, the pure nineteenth-century utilitarian, Muir has been described as an "aesthetic-utilitarian," a person who believes man of the twentieth century does not live by lumber (and sheep, and copper ore) alone.

In the 1920s the two young agencies developed parallel traditions of dedicated idealism, so similar in many respects that to the public at large a ranger was a ranger, a new species of American, an improved modern model of Natty Bumppo and the mountain men, to be admired by all, emulated by youth. The price for fervor was the rivalry between the agencies, so intense that in 1925 President Calvin Coolidge appointed a coordinating-mediating committee —which failed, leaving the rivalry unresolved, as it is to this day.

The objective eye saw virtues and faults on either side. The National Park Service soared in public esteem as Americans newly given the freedom of the wheel rushed to the national parks. Some critics, not fully understanding a comparatively weak agency's need to build a clientele by any possible means, felt the Park Service became so enamored of the crowds and their automobiles as to forget that "enjoyment" was supposed to leave the scene "unimpaired." Seemingly fearful of massive retaliation if it appeared too imperialistic, the Park Service resembled a gem collector so fastidious he will cherish only a single emerald or ruby or sapphire, the most magnificent of each; in 1923 the National Park Service opposed parks on

Baker and Adams and Olympus—because it already had Rainier.

As for the U.S. Forest Service, powerful though it was in the war against the Park Service, it was the underdog in a larger arena. Under Chief Forester William B. Greeley it retreated from the messianic belligerence of Pinchot into a prudent survivalism. Under Greeley the Forest Service gave up attacking the timber barons, who in exchange quit working to destroy the Forest Service. Death struggle evolved into symbiosis.

This was the politics of Washington City, not Washington State. In the Northwest, with so much Northern Pacific Land Grant and other timber in private hands, the typical "Old Ranger" during the first half of the century mainly walked around the country, following Indian and miner and sheepherder trails to see where they went, climbing peaks to see where he was, making maps and putting names on them so fire crews could be directed to blazes, installing signs at junctions and cutting a few logs and some brush, building fire lookout cabins on summits, and stringing wire along trails so lookouts could call in "smokes" to the ranger station on the handcrank telephone. The Old Ranger was chiefly a custodian, protector of the forest against fire and theft, the rangelands against overgrazing. Many of his generation went through their entire careers without participating in a timber sale.

The Old Ranger of the Forest Service got along amiably with his brethren in the Park Service. To be sure, the higher echelons of the former kept a wary eye on the latter, and guarded against preservationist aggressions by setting up such public relations barricades as its 1926 designation of a Mount Baker Park Division and, in 1931, the Glacier Peak–Cascade Recreation Unit.

However, no backcountry traveler who knew the Old Rangers was surprised that the first explicit governmental protection of wilderness was by the Forest Service. The Service's Aldo Leopold argued for wilderness as a place of refuge and restoration for civilized man, warning that "the existence of a wilderness-recreation famine has emerged as an incontrovertible fact." He influenced the Forest Service to set aside, in 1924, New Mexico's Gila Wilderness Area, a precedent as momentous in the history of the American earth as Yellowstone National Park.

The emergence of Leopold's philosophy even as Greeley's policy of prudent compromise rose to dominance is not the paradox it appears. The big lumbermen wished nothing better than to restrict access to public trees by their mosquitolike competitors, the little lumbermen who lacked a share of the forty million acres of the Northern Pacific Land Grant. The Forest Service after the compromise of Greeley had nothing to fear on the big-lumbermen front; on the other, against the Park Service, an appeal to the Muir soul as against the Pinchot belly was seen to be a valuable weapon. The Leopold-initiated L-20 Regulation of 1929, providing for "primitive areas" in which development and utilization were considerably restricted, made everybody at least content to simmer down and prepare for a distant confrontation. Unaware of all this devious reasoning, the backcountry traveler saw only that the Leopold initiative gave Washington State, in 1931, the Goat Rocks and Whatcom Primitive Areas—the latter expanded in 1935 to become the 801,000-acre North Cascades Primitive Area.

Students are not agreed as to whether a 1929 answer by the Forest Service to a question put by a member of The Mountaineers came from a hopeful supporter of Leopold or a hypocritical follower of Greeley: "In Washington there may be such areas set aside in the vicinity of the head of Lake Chelan, Glacier Peak...It is safe to say that the next many generations will in no way suffer from a lack of wilderness resources."

The years after 1933 seemed a time when preservationists could not lose. Franklin D. Roosevelt, the most committed of presidents to parks and wilderness, appointed as Secretary of the Interior the "old curmudgeon," Harold L. Ickes, as messianic and imperialistic as Pinchot himself. In 1933 Congress transferred the national monuments from the Forest Service to the Park Service, giving it—in the Olympics—a second responsibility in the state of Washington. Expanding the Park Service's vision, in

1937 Ickes masterminded a proposal for a 3.2-million-acre super-park encompassing the "Ice Peaks" of the Cascades from Canada to the Columbia River.

Ferdinand Silcox, who served FDR as Chief Forester, accepted Leopold as a legitimate contributor to a Forest Service policy more balanced and comprehensive than Greeley's. At FDR's suggestion, in 1937 Silcox appointed Robert Marshall as Chief of the Division of Recreation and Lands. Bob Marshall was a young forester from a wealthy New York family who in 1935 had joined Aldo Leopold in founding The Wilderness Society, which thereafter provided the movement with philosophical and political leadership. In 1939 the Forest Service superseded the L-20 Regulation with the more carefully considered and protective U Regulations, under which there could be (U-1) "wilderness areas" of one hundred thousand or more acres; (U-2) "wild areas" of five thousand to one hundred thousand acres; and (U-3) "recreation areas" of any size.

So enormous was the promise of the 1930s that the fruits seem meager. No national park was obtained in the North Cascades, at least in part because the park proposed by the short-lived Glacier Peak Association, founded in 1927, was submerged in 1939 by Marshall's proposal for a 795,000-acre Glacier Peak Wilderness. But the wilderness was not obtained either. Bob Marshall, who had been touring the West at a killing pace, drawing up proposals for protected areas, fell ill on his final breakneck Glacier Peak hike and in 1939 died, as did Ferdinand Silcox a few months later. These two premature deaths, and FDR's absorption in the war, ended the brief heyday of Leopold's ideas in the Forest Service.

It nevertheless was far from a lost decade. Conservationists, appalled at sequential reductions in the size of Mount Olympus National Monument, resolved to obtain more permanent protection. Culminating one of the longest struggles in the history of the American land, involving efforts by people from Seattle to New York (and very notably FDR himself), in 1938 Olympic National Park was established. Eventually it was expanded to nearly nine hundred thousand acres, even larger than envisioned by Wickersham and O'Neil during their trek across the Olympics forty-eight years earlier. Notoriously missing from the park, however, were the eastern ramparts of the range that overlook Puget Sound.

The 1940s were lean years indeed for wilderness proponents. In 1942 a final flicker in the Forest Service yielded the Mount Adams Wild Area which had meadows, rock, and ice, but no forests. For the rest of Bob Marshall's intentions for protection in the Northwest a regional parody of the U Regulations was devised, the "limited area" classification. This move was intended to quiet public controversy yet still allow the Forest Service to declassify limited areas with no discussion or even public notification, which it subsequently did. Indeed, the sole protective value of the limited status was that it provided conservationists with a fingernail clutch on the designated areas, a basis for asking embarrassing questions. When such questions were *not* asked, the limited areas vanished without a trace. In 1940 the North Cascades matter was disposed of with the preposterously small Glacier Peak Limited Area. In 1946 several other areas of contro-

Alpenglow on Mount Shuksan, North Cascades National Park

versy were "settled" with the Cougar Lakes, Alpine Lakes, Monte Cristo Peak, Packwood, and Mount St. Helens Limited Areas.

The establishment of Olympic National Park in 1938, half a century in the making, commenced in the forties what was to be (so far) half a century of defending: proposals were made in 1943, 1947, and 1953 to reduce the size of the park. In 1948 Olympic Park Associates was formed to spearhead the defense, as it continues to do because further attacks were launched in 1956, and 1966, and in the late 1970s.

The 1950s opened with the defense of another park, Rainier, where developers sought to transform Paradise Valley into a Sun Valley. The defense—successful—had the serendipitous effect of bringing together a mass of activist energy that quickly turned to other issues. The Mountaineers rebounded from the defensive to take the offensive at a pitch unmatched since the club's founding decade. Its longtime Northwest companion organizations similarly experienced a rejuvenation and soon were joined by a regional chapter of the Sierra Club and, in 1957, a new spearhead, the North Cascades Conservation Council.

The first area addressed was Glacier Peak, where the coalition began by innocently assuming that the Forest Service continued to honor the Leopold philosophy and intended to complete the Marshall initiative. A half-dozen years of discussions and negotiations ended in the final disillusionment of the last believer in the good intentions of the Forest Service. The passage by Congress in 1960 of the Multiple-Use-Sustained Yield Act, which Chief Forester McArdle (whose staff had written the act) said imposed the task of "converting old-growth timber stands to fast-growing young forests," merely confirmed what had become evident. The forest industry had just about finished shearing the trees from its Northern Pacific Land Grant and other booty lands and now wanted the national forests. The Old Ranger was retired. The custodial era of the Forest Service had ended.

The Glacier Peak controversy harshly spotlighted the resurgence of the Greeley philosophy. Unremittingly nagged by citizens, the Forest Service was unable to sweep the volcano and Bob Marshall under the rug and in 1960 designated a 458,505-acre Glacier Peak Wilderness, a bit more than half of the original Marshall proposal—and only brought up to even this inadequate size by the Secretary of Agriculture's decision to overrule the Forest Service's intentions to exclude the valleys of Agnes Creek and the Suiattle River.

The 1960s began with the preservation movement in Washington State at its strongest ever —and its angriest. The inadequacies of the Glacier Peak Wilderness plainly demonstrated that the new-style Forest Service would not protect entire natural units—low-valley forests together with highland flowers—but at most would grudgingly allow "wilderness on the rocks." In 1963, therefore, the citizens' coalition proposed a North Cascades National Park. Pundits were saying the national park movement was dead, that the two triumphs of the 1930s, Olympic and Kings Canyon, were the end of the line. They pointed to a quarter-century in which the only new national park was a little one in Puerto Rico, a gift of the Rockefellers.

The coalition did not believe the pundits. Two large-format books helped give impetus to the park movement. In 1964 The Mountaineers published *The North Cascades*, followed the next year by the Sierra Club's *The Wild Cascades: Forgotten Parkland.* Organizations across the nation lined up in support.

In Washington City the time was ripe. For the first time since President Roosevelt's energies were diverted to war, preservationist stalwarts in Congress had an ear in the White House. Without choosing sides in the boiling-up of the old interagency combat, President John F. Kennedy, in the "Treaty of the Potomac," appointed a joint Forest Service-Park Service North Cascades Study Team to review Glacier Peak-Mount Baker, the Alpine Lakes, and Cougar Lakes. In 1968 President Lyndon B. Johnson signed the North Cascades Act establishing a 504,500-acre North Cascades National Park, 105,000-acre Ross Lake National Recreation Area, 62,000-acre Lake Chelan National Recreation Area, and a 520,000-acre Pasayten Wilderness.

The acreages are impressive, a victory on the scale of the Olympic Park Act of 1938, and by rebutting the doomsayers it preserved for preservationists the Park Service alternative to the Forest Service—much to the latter agency's surprise, shock, dismay, and chagrin. However, many of those acres already were in the North Cascades Primitive Area, many others received only a "recreational area" status that has proven the more slippery with the years, and finally, only in part was it the park that had been sought. The preservationist proposal had meant to solve, at last, the Glacier Peak-Lake Chelan problem. The Forest Service was granted, as a consolation prize, the right to draw the boundaries of the park it had fought so long. Whether out of some devious motivation or from simple spite, the agency shifted the park northward and left the original problem still to be solved.

Another great—and flawed—victory of the sixties was the Wilderness Act of 1964, defining wilderness (in the language of Howard Zahniser, of The Wilderness Society) as a place where "the earth and its community of life are untrammeled by man, where man himself is a visitor who does not remain."

The 1964 act was not the Wilderness Bill first introduced in Congress in 1956, to be year after year bottled up in committee, largely at the behest of the mining industry. To attain passage and avoid a delay that might have proven fatal, the sponsors made compromises they hoped would be amended as time passed and the wilderness ethic grew more powerful. Twenty years later the compromises have not been amended, oil and gas and thermal-energy leases are imminent, and all the wilderness "won" in the past has to be defended all over again.

Nevertheless, the Wilderness Act of 1964 placed the Glacier Peak, Mount Adams, and Goat Rocks Wildernesses in the National Wilderness Preservation System from which they could not be deleted except by Congress. Until then the protection was purely at the pleasure of the Forest Service, which could declassify a wilderness—or any other of its administrative classifications—by the stroke of a pen. (This the service *did* in the case of its primitive areas

in the Olympic Mountains, once they had failed to serve their intended purpose of preventing establishment of Olympic National Park.)

Further, the 1964 legislation elevated Leopold's philosophy of wilderness to the federal statutes. Any federal lands, under any bureau, may be placed in the wilderness system. Portions of the national forests may be included, obviously—and the more wilderness the Forest Service must manage the more heirs of the Old Rangers it must tolerate within its fold.

Portions of the national parks also may be placed in the system, combining the guarantees of the 1916 National Park Act and the 1964 Wilderness Act—the highest protection that presently can be given the American earth. When current proposals are ultimately carried to completion, Washington will have three such doubly guarded areas.

Not since the 1930s had a decade opened with so much promise as the 1970s. The 1964 Wilderness Act had strengthened those in the Forest Service who embraced the vision of Leopold, and the 1968 North Cascades Act had frightened the many heirs of Greeley in the service. Preservationist spearhead groups proliferated. The Alpine Lakes Protective Society (ALPS) had adopted the area that had been "limited" in 1946 and proposed for wilderness since 1961. The Cougar Lakes Wilderness Alliance took responsibility for another limited area, also proposed for wilderness since 1961. Groups were organized to protect Mount St. Helens, Boulder River, Mount Baker, and the many other wildlands treated in Part III of this book. Discussions with the Forest Service were at a general level of civility unmatched for years—largely because the Forest Service to a considerable extent assigned negotiations to people who if not committed to Leopold were distinguished by a fair-minded consideration of competing demands. Hopes for wilderness were at their highest. Soon they would be dashed to their lowest. But first there was to be a great victory by which to remember the decade.

In 1971 The Mountaineers published its second "big issue book," *The Alpine Lakes*. One particular copy of this book may be the most persuasive single volume in wilderness history. In 1976 Congress passed the Alpine Lakes Bill

Lake Viviane and larch trees, Alpine Lakes Wilderness

and sent it to the White House. However, Congressman Joel Pritchard learned that the Bureau of the Budget had recommended a veto. In desperation he arranged a last-moment, five-minute White House appointment for Governor Dan Evans, who dropped everything and flew to Washington City. Governor Evans carried with him to the Oval Office a copy of *The Alpine Lakes*, hoping to flash a few scenes before the president's eyes. President Gerald Ford insisted on turning every page and lingering over each, ignoring the clock, exclaiming "It is such beautiful country! It must be saved!" And it was, because he signed into law the Alpine Lakes Wilderness.

So much for the good news of the 1970s. The bad news was that the timber industry decided, "Enough already." As indefatigably as the preservationists had pursued wilderness goals, lumbermen now strived for congressional passage of the Timber Supply Bill, which would compel national forests to be managed in the way of industry lands—a way Pinchot never would have permitted had he been given supervision of *all* American forests. Lumbermen appealed to the White House as well, and it became an almost annual event for the president to instruct the Forest Service to step up the pace of logging. Finally, the big timber companies that for half a century and more

21

had been content to let the Forest Service run on a long leash now began to shorten it up. Through the years the Forest Service had been distinguished by a large degree of decentralization: much independence was permitted the Regional Foresters by Washington City, the Forest Supervisors by the Regional Foresters, and the District Rangers by the Supervisors. Now the word went out from Washington City that the Forest Service was in the greatest danger since the embattled Pinchot years, when his successor, Greeley, saved the Service from annihilation by the timber industry by embarking on a policy of accommodation. The decision was made for another prudent retreat.

When the Forest Service undertook a nationwide Roadless Area Review and Evaluation (RARE) in 1971, preservationists fully cooperated, conceding the probable necessity of settling now, once and for all, which portions of the national forests were to be studied for possible wilderness designation, and which were to be devoted to multiple-use. However, when the results were released, preservationists were stunned. On reflection they saw that in its renewed fear of the timber industry the Forest Service had submerged its fear of the preservationists. Not even in the aftermath of the Marshall-Silcox deaths had it made so abrupt and radical a turnabout. As much in sorrow as anger the Sierra Club sued, and the courts ruled that RARE was illegal. The Forest Service retreated to the back rooms, came forth with RARE II—and it was worse—and was at length abandoned, leaving in its wake...chaos.

The intransigence expressed by the meager recommendations of RARE II spelled disaster for the remaining wildlands. Conservationists, fishermen, recreationists, and others came together to develop their own wilderness proposals and to take their case to Congress. This book seeks to bring to the attention of the people and lawmakers of the nation these various wilderness proposals for the state of Washington. If the agenda seems large, it is because the agendas of the past were never completed, were left to the future. The 1968 North Cascades Act did not finish the job for Glacier Peak, Lake Chelan, Mount Baker, or the Pasayten. The 1938 creation of Olympic National Park left much to do there. Even the establishment of Mount Rainier National Park failed to protect the whole of The Mountain. The Cougar Lakes, Boulder River, Salmo-Priest, Juniper Forest, and so many others have *everything* left to do.

• • •

As this book is published it is twenty years since the Wilderness Act, the same span between the Seattle of 1,107 residents and of 42,837, between the Washington Territory of the North West Boundary Survey and the Washington State of the closing of the frontier. The changes in the Washington earth during these last twenty years are comparable to those of the long-ago twenty years. Indeed, in some instances they will be more long-lasting—on the human measure of time, virtually permanent.

Year by year people living in the Puget Sound lowlands have watched clearcuts climb their western and eastern horizons. The forest industry has ascended from the Western Hemlock Zone, where it has worked a century and a quarter, into the Pacific Silver Fir Zone, with a different mix of species and a very different climate, which ecologists are only beginning to understand, and higher still into the Mountain Hemlock Zone which is bounded by alpine meadows.

When the industry began its climb to the summits in the 1950s it was buttressed by the overconfidence of a forestry that was as much a faith as a science. Mountain travelers recall from that time the Forest Service's first high-country clearcuts, and the proud signs erected beside roads, "Logged 1951, Planted 1952." Rangers have gone about removing such signs, embarrassed that a third of a centry later hundreds of these clearcuts are growing nothing bigger than fireweed and vine maple.

The industry has ceased bothering to claim it can "farm" trees as high as trees can grow. A hiker who counts the rings in a stump atop a 4,000-foot ridge and determines that a tree eighteen inches in diameter was three hundred years old when cut knows he is not on a tree farm, but a tree mine. When the hiker tells this to a company forester, the answer is not outraged protest but a shrug of the shoulders. "Talk to the comptroller. Bottom-line forestry, it's called. Down low we grow trees. Up high we just cut 'em. After all, if there were lumps of gold scattered around we'd not let 'em lay just because we don't have an alchemist on the payroll to make gold from granite."

The bottom line is regularly and candidly and publicly explained by the president of a major timber company. In his standard speech he points out that his firm and others will finish "liquidating their inventory" of virgin forests in Washington by 1990 or so. The second-growth forests on their lands will not come to full production until far into the twenty-first century. His company's projections for operations in the next half-century include the forests of the Suiattle and Agnes Creek, the Big Beaver and the Ashnola and Pasayten, and the Hoh and the Queets and the Quinault. Instead of managing for a sustained yield of timber on their own lands, industry intends to chainsaw the public lands.

An officer of another large timber company has further elucidated the bottom line. At a public hearing where his firm was accused of logging so irresponsibly that rains were stripping the mountainsides of soil, he angrily responded, "What business is it of *yours*? We *own* the land. It's *our* soil. If we wanted to dig it up and truck it to California it wouldn't be any of *your* concern!"

"We own the land..."

The man who made this statement had been living on the Washington earth perhaps half a century. Many of the trees his company was cutting were a dozen human lifetimes old when his ancestors came to America. The fish that his company's bulldozers and trucks had driven out of the rivers belonged to races that had been swimming those waters since the melting of the Pleistocene ice. The soil the clearcutting was flushing down the rivers was the sum product of perhaps fifty eons of weathering.

The industry bottom line typically summarizes the current year, scans the next decade, glances at the next half-century; beyond that, the void. The industry invested in science when it hoped chemistry and genetics would vastly increase profits; now it mainly invests in technology, the better in the age of the helicopter and balloon to pluck the lumps of green gold from precipices.

The bottom line of the Forest Service must be different, for it is required to have a broader, societal view. It must remember Pinchot's "long run" and Leopold's plea for wilderness as a place of refuge. The National Park Act, the Wilderness Act, are preliminary ventures into a new body of law, the law of the centuries ahead.

The American people have come to that understanding, even if the Forest Service has not. They see that humanity is pressing the limits of Earth and is threatening to make it unlivable. The realization is dawning that a new ethic is needed, one of living together with the land and its living creatures. Preservation of our wildlands is a part of that ethic.

◆ ◆ ◆

PART II
Where Man Is A Visitor

ON THE DRAGON SHORE

It isn't the sound that awakens, the sound
that has been there all the night and forever,
but its distance, reminding of a minus tide
that won't wait for dreams. The June morning begins with making the day's first tracks
in virgin sand, out from the driftwood to the
start of the rock shelf, roots of a vanished
sea stack, open to the sky only a few hours
a year. Sunrays streaming over the sea-bluff
forest warm the back of bare legs as breezes
stirred by the surf chill the front. The route
leads over hillocks and ribs of crusty bar-
nacles and slippery weedery, by pools of green
anemones and pink and purple sea stars and
orange algae, along channels where broken
waves are sloshing and mother seals are
teaching pups to hunt. The way ends on a
jutting prow in a glow of salt mist from
breakers exploding their pulses of wind-energy
from far out in the Oceane Sea, the name
given by mariners of old who thought there
was only one, continuous from Europe to the
Indies.

Back at the driftwood kitchen the pancakes are in the frying pan, to be soaked in
spruce-tip syrup boiled up from new growth
of a tree that leans over the beach and has
no more than another winter before the
storms pull it down.

The low tide has set the boots marching
south, marching north, the parade of pilgrims
comes from across America to where wilderness of the land meets wilderness of the
ocean. Despite heavy packs they walk fast,
striving to know as much ocean as they can
on a short vacation.

The pilgrims at the pancake kitchen have
rounded only enough rock-jumbled points,
climbed over only enough jungled headlands,
to escape automobiles and motels, dune bug-
gies and surfboards. Here they have settled
down to *see*, understanding as they do the
ocean *is* one, and the more of it walked by
in a day the less can be known.

The feet of the see-ers are now bootless,
to feel sand in the toes, important. There is
much to keep an eye on: the snag atop an
offshore sea stack, the nest of a pair of bald
eagles, most impressive birds of summer, and
of winter too, with the sometime exception
of snowy owls driven by hunger from the
Arctic and finding no lemmings here, either.
There is surf to watch lest a remarkable
wave be missed, unprecedented in all past
eons, not to be repeated in eons ahead.

The tide is on the flood, blocking the
easy walk-arounds of points, and the pancakes are too heavy to carry up and over
tunnels in headland salal. A book is taken
to a driftwood nook sheltered from sun and
breeze. Pancakes are nestled in the sand.
Words blur on the page. Eyes close.

The nearness of the sound awakens. The
rumble is benign, not as in winter when
violent crash-booms make the heart skip.
Green summer waves roll smoothly over the
submerged rock shelf, smash to white
smithereens on the sand. Foam glides hissing
to the nook and the bubbles wink out, not
as in winter when they mass in billows of
wind-quivering spindrift, said of old to be the
flesh of mermaids dead in the storm.

Overleaf - Ten Peaks Range, Glacier Peak Wilderness

Eroded rock in the coastal strip, Olympic National Park

27

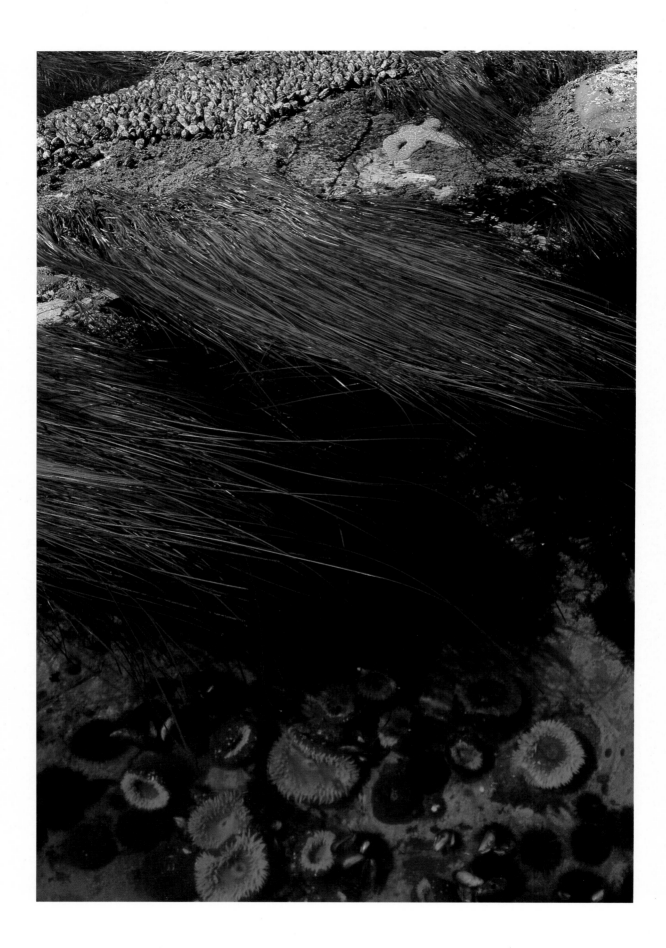

The high tide has halted the boot parade, giving privacy sufficient to fling off clothes and splash through the slurry of cold water and sand and weed. Ankles get wet, next knees, and then a wave curls over the head and collapses, tumbling toes in the air and nose in the deep; eyes open to briefly see the Oceane Sea in the way of the hunting seals and the hunted fish.

A dozen turmoils goosepimple the skin and chatter the teeth. A sit in the sun tingle-dries the body enough to don clothes, the minimum to avoid embarrassing sunburns.

Back at the kitchen the scavengers are assembling, the amateur hunter-gatherers who have lightly cropped the wildland to know it the better, not merely seeing and hearing and smelling but tasting, and to know a little about the people who lived here twelve thousand years, cropping so gently they *could* live here that long. One amateur has captured a crab in a trap of sticks and string, others have dug clams from gravel and plucked mussels from rocks, gathered seaweed and miner's lettuce, still another has brought out the snakebite remedy and the snake and announced the happy hour with blasts on a kelp horn. During the sipping of clam nectar and seaweed soup, the crunching of wildland salad and the dipping of clams and mussels in lemon-butter, the gazing to buttresses of the stack where the colony of sea lions has

returned from a day of hunting, and to the lowering sun, it is sagely commented to nods of agreement that everything is *just right.*

The tide is on the ebb and there is deep contentment in knowing the chief duty of the see-er has been done, watching the tide come in, the tide go out.

The campfire brightens as the sun cools to a wizened ember that at nine o'clock touches the water, setting off a pink and orange and crimson sizzling along the western horizon. At ten o'clock the first star twinkles in the darkening blue, ending a day of eighteen hours, compensation on these northern shores for the meager eight hours of winter.

The bedroom is in the spruce forest, on a terrace several feet higher than the driftwood line. In the night the tide again floods, almost to the kitchen. But the nearing of the sound barely half-awakens, only enough for remembering how it is in the city, when newly home from the ocean, to awake frightened by the loss of the pulse, and for remembering how it is in a winter storm to not sleep at all for listening to thousands of tons of logs hurling against the spruce forest, battering the defenses of the continent. Within that horrifying roar is something more than wood and water and wind. Mariners returning from voyages on the Oceane Sea told stories of ship-eating dragons. *True* stories.

Tidepool, Olympic National Park

The Olympics

OLYMPIC NATIONAL PARK: THE COAST

North from the Hoh River to Quateata, the Quileute River to Cape Alava, and the Ozette River to Point of Arches and Shi Shi Beach—more than forty miles as the bald eagle flies and the gray whale swims—wilderness of the ocean meets wilderness of the land. A surf ranked among the world's most violent ceaselessly advances into the continent, cutting off islands and sea stacks, nesting and resting places for birds and mammals protected in national wildlife refuges.

On Cape Alava, westernmost point in the old forty-eight states, the Makah people over the centuries repeatedly rebuilt a village that as repeatedly was overwhelmed by mud slides, which in destroying homes preserved artifacts that now provide the fullest existing record of the recent and remote past of human residence on the coast.

Surprisingly, and irrationally, the beach below the high-tide line is not in the national park. Under state jurisdiction and lacking wilderness designation, the beach is subject to airplane and powerboat intrusion, to motorcycles illegally pioneering routes across the narrow park strip to get to it, and could even be leased

Shi Shi Beach and Point of Arches, Olympic National Park

Overleaf - *Lost River Valley, Olympic National Park*

Cameron Basin,
Olympic National Park

for commercial purposes. In the past few years the "wilderness beach" has so grown in fame as to draw hikers from throughout America and the world. But the wildness is not fully guaranteed, not yet.

OLYMPIC NATIONAL PARK

"Washington has her great unknown land like the interior of Africa," declared the governor of the brand-new state in 1889, the year before the frontier was pronounced officially dead. The existence of so large an expanse of wilderness so near their homes was a source of much curiosity and pride among residents of the young cities in the shadow of the peaks. This being "the last wilderness," where the American frontier ran out of continent to conquer, it became a national concern, leading to the creation of a forest reserve in 1897, a national monument in 1909, and a national park in 1938.

In 1979 it became an international concern, designated by the United Nations as part of the World Heritage and Biosphere Reserve. Many languages are heard on park trails, spoken by foreign visitors among the two million a year who come to see the unique combination of wilderness ocean, temperate rain forests, alpine meadows, and glaciers.

The park also is among the world's greatest wildlife refuges, spacious enough to comprehend the complete summer-winter ranges of animal communities that live out their lives free from human management, truly wild. Indicative of the natural balance, the park is believed to be home for more cougar than any other area of comparable size.

33

Lichen and stonecrop,
Olympic National Park

OLYMPIC PENINSULA

Olympic National Park, a half-century in the making, never was finished. Lumbermen and the U.S. Forest Service fought to prevent creation of the park, and though failing in that, were able to dictate the maximum size. Working under a limit on the number of acres they could protect, park proponents felt they had to meet the most immediate threat—to the rain forests of the Hoh, Bogachiel, and Queets. They were forced to omit the valleys and ridges most accessible and popular recreationally, confident that the following generation would add them.

It has not been done. For a quarter-century the view of the Olympics from the cities of Puget Sound has been relentlessly transformed from the deep green of virgin forest to the brown mange of clearcuts. Ridges have been logged to the crest. Trails have been converted to motorcycle roads. The winter ranges of elk,

bear, deer, and cougar are threatened, as is the water quality of streams that support valuable runs of steelhead and coho, pink, and chum salmon.

From the rain forests of Colonel Bob country to the rainshadow tundra of the Gray Wolf; from the Canal-Front valleys of the Skokomish, Hamma Hamma, Duckabush, Dosewallips, Quilcene, and Dungeness to the summits of The Brothers and the cirque basins of the Mildred Lakes, the task needs finishing— the task of wilderness protection set forth by Judge Wickersham and Lieutenant O'Neill during their expedition across the Olympics in July of 1890.

Evening reflection, Mildred Lakes,
Olympic National Forest

Hoh Rain Forest, Olympic National Park

35

POLE OF REMOTENESS

The plan was to sit tight in Seattle until the onset of the Midwinter Clear, a meteorological phenomenon the wise men said was an invariable annual event, occurring sometime between Santa Claus and the Easter Bunny. By so waiting we would avoid the fate of the many groups of our friends who had set off on fixed dates and spent days floundering in rain-forest rain, dodging widow-makers and flying moss. I always greeted them cheerfully when they returned, wrinkled up like prunes, and was full of smart remarks, since nothing in my life plan was more certain than that I never would attempt the first winter ascent of Mount Olympus.

Eventually I did sign on for a trip, as a favor to a friend who needed a third person to meet a Park Service requirement. I rested easy, long since having wised up about Santa Claus and the Easter Bunny and the Midwinter Clear. Nobody ever went broke betting against good weather on Olympus, winter *or* summer.

Well, subsequently I took to hanging my Christmas stocking with care and putting out a bunch of carrots Easter eve, because *the Clear came.*

I should explain that in the period of these events I was rapidly reverting to my natural condition of valley-pounder and ridge-runner, increasingly hostile to any peak that demanded I soil my hands on it. However, I continued to be a devout "semiexpeditioner," meaning I understood why Mallory and Smythe and Shipton did what they did, but I wasn't English and thus couldn't go to Everest and so did what was possible locally, on short time and short cash, to escape. The "Washington pole of remoteness"—the spot in the state the farthest from downtown Seattle—fascinated me the way the South Pole did Robert Falcon Scott. Queets Basin, Luna Cirque, they were my sort of place.

I knew, of course, the *true* pole of remoteness was somewhere in winter, when wilderness expands by several orders of magnitude. The reason I didn't do much winter mountaineering was snow. In summer, in amounts proportionate to other elements of the landscape, it's exceedingly picturesque and excellent for cold drinks. In winter, however, it gets completely out of hand.

Part of my distaste was due to the primitive condition of our technology, which hadn't advanced very far beyond inventing the wheel. In winter you had to be busy, busy, busy all the time, less in hopes of ever getting really comfortable than to avoid freezing to death. Vilhjálmur Stefánsson, who stuck it to the Englishmen (whose polar expeditions always ended in disaster) by writing a book called *The Friendly Arctic,* said, "An adventure is a sign of incompetence." The wilderness is more exciting if you don't know too much or own too much. Well, there are other things in life besides excitement.

Monday night, January 29, we drove from Seattle to the end of the Hoh River road, arriving after midnight. The ranger, bless his heart, got up to greet us and let us sleep in the bunkhouse—unheated. I thought the thermometer on the wall must be broken and wondered if it was the chattering of my teeth that did it.

I had to admit that Tuesday was a champion of a day, the Clear gleaming blue through the giant trees, bands of elk tromping and chomping around in the snow. The

Mount Olympus, Olympic National Park

temperature was twenty degrees—in the sun, when it managed to push a ray through the cathedral roof. It wasn't a whole lot warmer inside our Khaki Gang costumes of Army packs, Army parkas, Army boots, Army mittens and socks and long-handled underwear. We had Army feather bags so we wouldn't necessarily die in our sleep, but a breather on the trail was risky—you could feel your blood sludging and brain turning silly. The good thing was that we were able to carry the Army beavertails on our backs and walk the whole fifteen valley miles on a rain crust solid as concrete. At dusk we reached the

Elk Lake shelter, where some saint had left a stack of dry wood that let us get as deliriously warm as Sam McGee at his cremation.

Wednesday we started up the slope, ran out of rain crust and put on snowshoes, and soon took them off as the angle steepened. On a route that in summer is an easy trail, we roped up, chopped steps in icicles, and belayed over avalanche chutes, too busy to pay much attention to the gray sheet sliding across the sky from the south. So much for the Clear.

At Glacier Meadows we glissaded down a snow wall into an icebox—a brand-new lean-to shelter—and shoveled and stomped and scraped most of the afternoon, trying to bring the accommodations up to the minimum for survival. When we'd done everything possible, we had an hour left before the end of the world and snowshoed through frosted Christmas trees in snow as airy as talcum powder to the edge of the Blue Glacier.

The glacier *was* blue in the twilight, and so were the glazed cliffs and the icefall, and the clouds rushing north a mile a minute, beheading the peaks of Olympus and lowering onto the Snow Dome. Even the wind felt blue.

I had recently seen *Scott of the Antarctic*, the greatest expedition film ever made, and in this gale on Olympus could hear the gale over the South Pole—and Vaughan William's music—and the words Scott had written in his journal on January 17, forty-one years earlier: "The Pole...Great God! This is an awful place..."

Snow began blasting from the Pole. We snowshoed back to the lean-to and slid down in our hole and managed to set frozen squaw wood to smoldering enough to strangle and blind us and eventually to cook what Scott would have called "a fat Polar hoosh in spite of our chagrin"—chicken noodle soup and corned beef, with chunks of pumpernickel and butter. A restaurant that could duplicate the dish would make a fortune. If it could draw enough customers to such a place. Because the place was the secret ingredient, of course.

Thursday morning we banqueted on a pot of oatmeal and prunes and Eagle Brand condensed sweetened milk. With the wheezing and the weeping, that occupied the morning. At noon we opened khaki tins of Army miscalled pemmican and drank cocoa with marshmallows and Eagle Brand. I decided that if I somehow ever had to go hiking in winter again I'd make darn sure to take plenty of Eagle Brand.

Combined with the smoke it impelled us out into the blizzard—not to attempt an ascent, purely for the exercise—and onto the Blue Glacier—blue no more—pure white underfoot and overhead and all around. We couldn't see each other, only the rope stretching off in the white void.

Why were we here?

On the last January 17 of his life Scott wrote in his journal, "Well, it is something to have got here..."

The gale roared on, and I wondered if the avalanche chutes on the trail were roaring yet. Until we crossed them and descended to the big trees it was a waste to discuss what-all we'd put on our hamburgers in Queets, how many pitchers of beer we'd drink in Seattle. Olympus wasn't in the same space-time as Seattle. Or Queets. Or the nice ranger at the end of the Hoh road. It was as far away as I'd ever been, and probably farther than I had any need to be.

Thursday night there was more smoke and hoosh and blizzard. It was a happy little hole in the snow, but not so happy we didn't have a few thoughts about home. The soonest we could be there, with luck, was Saturday or Sunday. The ranger, and our support party in Seattle, had been told not to worry until Wednesday or Thursday or so. That didn't mean *we* couldn't, a little.

DISCOVERY

In the cool of the July morning the Big Red Truck halted at the end of the road, Bark Shanty Shelter. The two dozen twelve- and thirteen-year-olds, the several midteenagers, and the college-age leader jumped to the ground and lifted down packs consisting of personal gear and shares of the group's food rolled up in wool sleeping bags and lashed on packboards—Trapper Nelsons, dish racks, and string packs. Toilet rolls were impaled on packboard horns, Number Ten cans tied outside. Boot soles were studded with slivers, rosebuds, hobs, and calks, short pants were rolled up to the crotch, cups were hooked to belts. The line of Scouts walked away from the truck and road into the forest tunnel, deep in the green, far from the sun, and marched to the clank of the Ten Cans.

The twelve- and thirteen-year-olds, many smaller than their packs, knew only what they'd been told by the big kids—that during the three days they would see three rivers and two passes and no cars and no people— except at the top where the candy store by the highway at Marmot Pass sold ice cream cones and soda pop.

Before this reward there was to be the testing. In the afternoon, at Shelter Rock, the Scouts drank from the Big Quilcene River. The path turned steeply up from forest to brush and rock open to the punishing sun, not a bit of shade for a rest, never a trickle to dissolve the glue in the mouth. Big kids told little kids to pick up a pebble and suck it. That was the Scout way. The Big Quilcene was remembered.

Here on the dreaded Poopout Drag the limits were found. Collapsed kids were passed with sympathy, not contempt, for each survivor still able to stagger onward under a

Alpine meadow,
Olympic National Forest

39

pack as heavy as the sun felt the nearness of limits, knew another collapse might come, and soon.

The big kids steamed ahead to Camp Mystery, at timberline, to build the supper fire. Little kids were set to work on arrival stirring Ten Cans, scorching hands and bare legs, strangling on smoke. Big kids ran back down the trail to fetch the packs of poop-outs, and the party assembled for supper. Each was served a cup of rice and canned salmon, a half-cup of chocolate pudding, and as much tea as was wanted to fill up on.

They let the fire go out to conserve wood. The pooped crawled in wool bags open to the sky and shivered. Those who could move about at all went walking to keep warm. Big kids ran in gangs up Iron Mountain. Little kids loitered singly up the trail.

The path opened out in green lawns dotted by shrubs, such a landscape as would demand the full-time Saturday toil of hundreds of kids. However, these lawns and shrubs had not been planted as an adult plot against the freedom of the young. Yet neither had they been mowed and trimmed by rangers, as everyone suspected was done at Rainier's Paradise Valley in midweek, when the tourists weren't around.

The day had begun where the river ran through tangled underbrush and tall trees of virgin forest, never touched by a logger. It was ending where a creek ran through lawns and shrubs that took care of themselves. Then the creek stopped! Or rather started, in a gush from beneath a rock. Books told how explorers had spent years searching for the Sources of the Nile. In a single day the Scouts—one, at least—had found the Source of the Big Quilcene.

The trail climbed through fields of flowers, such a vastness of blossoming as to make a kid tremble in loathing. However, here there was no need for Saturdays to be spent on knees, weeding. Here the plants got along together without fussing. There weren't

any bad plants to be punished and exterminated. Up here even the weeds were flowers.

The scene was familiar. But the memories were not of earlier trips to Paradise Valley. This was completely different—because of the river that shrank to a creek, the forest that gave way to a garden, the pack as big as a Scout, the hot sun of the Poopout Drag, the eight miles of trail and 4,000 feet of elevation gain, the pebble sucked until it nearly dissolved. This was as different from the parking-lot and picnic-table meadows of Paradise as it was from home—yet it felt homelike. Not the city home, the waking-life home. A home where castles would be no surprise, gnomes could be peering from boulders, witches and giants and ogres lurking in ambush, where princesses and princes might come skipping through the grass.

The trail climbed to the sky, pink and orange and yellow. A post held a sign, "Marmot Pass, 6000 feet." As the little kids had begun to suspect halfway up the Poopout Drag, there was no highway, no candy store.

The sun had fallen behind black peaks in the west. The Dungeness valley, below, lay deep in night. The sky was of colors that had no names and cast a strange radiance on rock-barren ridges and tiny flowers and Scouts, who felt themselves turning into characters in fairy tales and adventure stories.

To be a Scout was to dream of adventure, to read about explorers braving the wilderness. Wilderness was the jungles of Africa and the Amazon, mountains of Tibet, frozen wastes of the Poles. Wilderness was where Scouts would go when they grew up to be adventurers. It wasn't where they lived. In this year of 1938 the wilderness of Washington was as long gone as great-great-grandparents. Or so the Scouts had supposed.

Now, at Marmot Pass, they gazed down into wilderness and west into wilderness. It was *here*. They were *in it*. They didn't mind that there was no ice cream or soda pop.

The San Juans

SAN JUAN ISLANDS NATIONAL WILDLIFE REFUGE

Strewn across the Inland Sea between Vancouver Island and the Washington mainland are the peaks and ridges of a submerged mountain range, the San Juan Islands. Some of the more than three hundred isles are large enough for human population, year-round or summer, but many are scarcely more than rock summits barely poking above salt water. Seventy-odd, ranging downward in size from 145-acre Matia Island to the likes of 10-acre Puffin Island and others that would require several to make a single acre, have been given wilderness protection under management of the U.S. Fish and Wildlife Service. Inhospitable to people, with a sparse cover of low-growing plants and a scattering of shrubby trees, they are much appreciated by seabirds and shorebirds. More than two hundred species regularly visit, nest, or feed in the ringing waters, joined there by river otters, seals, and one of the largest populations of killer whales—orcas—in North America.

Sunset from Matia Island, San Juan Islands Wilderness

Mount Baker from Matia Island

SHADES OF GREEN

The color of Washington wilderness is rock gray and ice white and flower bright. Dominantly, though, it is tree green, the many shades of green of a multitude of diverse forest communities, perhaps more—and more various—than anywhere else on the planet.

The world's largest expanse of temperate coniferous forests, its greatest accumulation of biomass, centers on Western Washington. The Sitka Spruce Zone fronts the ocean with tough thickets of the tree that thrives on winter gales and summer fogs and buffeting surf. Where given a chance, in the comparative calm of the Olympic valleys, it grows huge and tall.

East of the Olympics the sea-level forests are in the Western Hemlock Zone, this and the western red cedar being the climax species, Douglas fir their chief associate. All three attain giant size and great age—the biggest and oldest specimens of the species—as can be seen in the Grove of the Patriarchs of Mount Rainier National Park, in the remnant old-growth of the Greenwater River, and in a number of other places: not a large number because only a few ancient stands have not been converted to lumber, shakes, and pulp, replaced by "tree farms" where no forest ever will grow old, or even middle-aged.

Next higher is the Pacific Silver Fir Zone, named for its climax species, a tree of the snow country that remains deep in winter long after flowers are blooming in lowlands. On a spring evening as the climber plunge-steps homeward from his peak, down through the snow, the silver-white bark reflects the day lingering in the sky and suffuses the forest with a soft inner light.

Highest is the Mountain Hemlock Zone, where the forest opens out in a mosaic of tree clumps and subalpine meadows. Alaska cedar jungles cliffs. Knolls are crowned by subalpine fir, the classic Christmas tree.

Variations on these and other basic themes are myriad throughout Western Washington. The Olympic rain forest might better be called a fog forest, abundant as it is in epiphytes, plants that grow on other plants not as parasites but independently drinking the atmosphere; the fog feeds the club moss heavily draping the branches of big-leaf maples and the licorice fern growing a hundred feet up the trunks. It might as accurately be called an elk forest, since the heavy chomping by bands of the big beasts keeps the floor open and parklike, rather than becoming a tangle impenetrable to any creature larger than a mosquito.

The "nearly rain forest" of such valleys as Barclay Creek and the Boulder River lack elk and ocean fogs; however, the deep-shadowed mountain clefts brew their own mists, nourishing the mosses and lichens and ferns and liverworts and molds that urge a hiker to hurry his lunch before it turns green.

Stream-terrace forests of western red cedar have an effect on the viewer perhaps only less dumbfounding than the giant sequoia of the Sierra. Their enormous masses of precious wood, lodes richer than any gold ever found in the state, have been mostly mined out. Of the few remaining forests, the most celebrated is in the valley of Big Beaver Creek, which preservationists spent fifteen years defending—in the end successfully—against Seattle City Light's attempt to drown the cedars by raising Ross Dam.

The West Side story in Washington is deep green, twilight at noon, and scarcely any open space except water and glaciers. The East Side story is brilliant green, sun early and sun late, sun in the summer and sun in the winter, and *two* timberlines, the lower at the warm-dry end of the climatic scale, the upper at the cold-wet.

Red-cedars in Big Beaver Valley

Ponderosa pine, Okanogan Highlands   *Silver fir, Olympic Mountains*

The Juniper Forest downwind of the Columbia River sands is unique among the lower-timberline communities, the groves of western juniper, here at the northernmost reach of the species, intermingled with a true desert of marching dunes, the state's finest.

The tree that epitomizes Eastern Washington's lower forests, in the zone bordered by sagebrush steppe, is the ponderosa pine. The species grows—very slowly—to impressive size, aided by periodic brushfires that merely charcoal the bark of the big pines but kill the scrub that competes for scarce water. Until a quarter-century ago, tourists could readily view superb roadside specimens; most have since fallen to the miners. Old trees survive on trails—where trails survive. The hiker from the West Side, where the most dangerous poison is in the barbs of the devil's club, is particularly struck by the beauty of the ponderosa because usually he is listening for a rattling menace in the stirrings of the green grass and often thinks he sees, in the brown-orange-black bark of the pine, the *geist* of a great gaudy snake.

The most-loved tree of the East Side's upper forests is the evergreen that is not, the larch. It is also the tree—in both species, western and Lyall's—that takes the longest to know. The acquaintance is best begun in winter, seeing starkly black, evidently dead trunks and limbs; continued in spring, amazed by the miracle of rebirth, fresh green needles budding; and perfected in autumn as the first snows whiten the highlands, the needles turning yellow and orange, the low sun igniting whole mountainsides, and photographers thronging.

Life-in-death is a recurring theme on the East Side. The snow-eating Chinook wind sends hell-roaring floods down the valleys, ripping out conifers, opening room for the cottonwood and aspen that—with the larch and mountain ash and dogwood and vine maple and big-leaf maple and bitter cherry and Indian plum and willow and serviceberry—stage the most brilliant fall-color extravaganza west of New England.

During the dry years of the 1920s lightning torched off summer-long fires that

Douglas-fir, Olympic National Forest

Vine maple, Alma Copper area

Western hemlock, Boulder River Area

burned hundreds of square miles of Pasayten and Okanogan country. A hiker of today walks for hours through stands of spindly lodgepole pine, the species that is pioneering amid silver forests dead a half-century and never lovelier, then emerges in parkland where bleached sculptures mingle with black-green cones of Englemann spruce and ethereal billows of pale green Lyall's larch.

Lightning also transforms the bushy trunks of the whitebark pine into contorted skeletons that are picked clean by sun, wind, frost, birds, and insects. Hikers who see such a relic atop a rock promontory against the background of a towering cumulonimbus with a heart black as night may wonder how *they* would look after being set ablaze on a stormy afternoon and left out for decades to silver under the sky.

The highest East Side forests are composed of the "alpine-horizontal" races of subalpine fir, western white pine, Alaska cedar, and Rocky Mountain juniper. These form the krummholz, the elfinwood, which often borders the felsenmeer, the rock sea, where the lichens grow, Earth's longest-lived communities.

There are trees smaller than elfin. In September a hiker who sits by a glacial stream meandering a tundra basin and lowers her eyes to the ground will find there—racing for species-perpetuation against winter—willows an inch tall, each tiny tree putting out a gray pussy larger than it is.

47

THE GOOD SLEEP

Eyes expecting motel furniture opened to golden light on brown cliff and white snow. In the click of four synaptic relays he, first, didn't know where he was; knew but thought it a dream; knew it was real and supposed he'd been transported by magic; then remembered leaving the road by flashlight, climbing through a night of vast, dim presences, hearing the welcome-home roar of an ice avalanche on the mile-high cliffs of Mount Johannesburg, and unrolling the bag on soft humus.

Another click and he realized no telephone would be jangling him to attention in

Walla Walla or Corvallis or Pocatello or Bozeman or Saskatoon, commanding him to flap his wings to Spokane or Salt Lake City or San Francisco or New York.

Already his face was bristly and hair tangled, his body that for months had been showered and deodorized and pent in suit and tie and button-down shirt and shiny oxfords was fermenting the sweat of the night hike into a mellow wildland stink.

He slipped his glasses on to bring The Triplets into focus, sunrays flooding over Cascade Pass onto the east walls of the summit ribs. He crawled out of the bag and wandered barefoot, cold flowers in his toes, listening to waterfalls from the hanging glaciers, hearing far-below rivers running west to saltchuck and east to sagebrush. He considered putting on boots and setting off at high speed in all directions. Then he reflected he already was where he wanted to go. He crawled back in the bag, into dreams.

Not dreams of past or future, the distant or fanciful. Dreams of sun on rock of The Triplets and ice of Johannesburg, of blue sky and falling water, of breezes flowing over his cheek, mountain hemlocks shadowing his bed.

This was not a sleep for the body. It was a sleep for the year of unfree sleeps in motels and hotels and airplanes and conference rooms, sleeps subject to interruption by the telephone that chained him to the whims of the million-odd Americans who had his number, sleeps subject to annihilation by the alarm clock that remorselessly ticked off the lost minutes and hours and days.

Now and then he let himself float near enough the surface to gather in sights and sounds that he then took back down for seeing and hearing by the dreaming eye and ear. The sleep stopped time and caught the place and held it as fixed as a specimen under a microscope for examination by the dreaming mind in a moment as indivisible as eternity.

The ribs of The Triplets glowed pink on the east, shone brilliantly on the north, flushed rose red on the west, and the dream made them one. But at last the dream saw the three illuminations were a day. Time resumed.

In twilight he climbed the meadows and screes of Mixup Arm to the Cache Glacier, where millions of tiny black ice worms had surfaced to feed on algae. He scrambled from snow to the flowers of Cache Col just as they went dark in the shadow of a jutting buttress of Johannesburg. A buck, startled, leapt high into tawny sunlight, fell to gray shadow, rebounded over the roll of the slope, and was last seen diving to the Middle Fork Cascade River thousands of feet below, going down in flames.

The hiker dropped his pack at Kool-Aid Lake. Night had climbed from valley forests to highland meadows, to glaciers and cliffs. The pink glow lingered on the summits of Johannesburg and Formidable, then faded, and the western sky darkened to let the stars come out.

Tree-shrubs on the brink of the tundra shelf beside the waterfall outlet, boulders dumped by the old glacier or tumbled from cliffs of Magic and Hurryup, gained the fluidity of shadows. The hour had come when trees can walk and rivers talk. Sleep would not be deep here, alone among the sly sneakings, the whispers and murmurs and chuckles. But this sleep, too, would be good for what ailed him.

View from Cascade Pass, North Cascades National Park

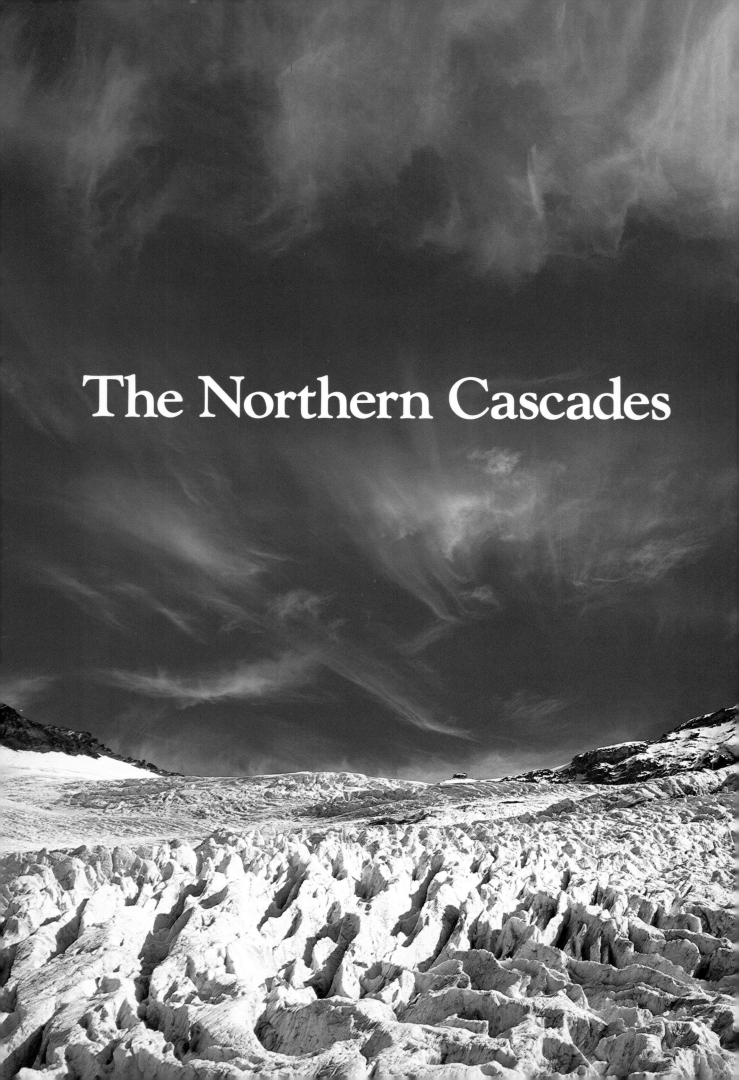

The Northern Cascades

MOUNT BAKER COUNTRY

In a wintry dawn climbers on Mount Baker's glaciers see its shadow cast far across forests and farms and cities and salt-waterways to Vancouver Island. Komo Kulshan, the local folk called it, the Great White Watcher. So raptly was it watched by so many that in the 1920s the U.S. Forest Service designated a "Mount Baker Park Division"—but less to protect the volcano than the Service's control of the land.

In 1968 a true park was created, the North Cascades National Park. However, it was mostly rock and ice, with few forests—and none of Baker's forests, or even its rock and ice. Logging trucks ascended from valley bottoms nearly to the meadows. Snowmobiles were loosed on the glaciers.

The Watcher's hinterland has been treated as badly or worse. The Twin Sisters to the west, their iron-rusty ridges a striking contrast to Baker's white, their valleys harboring a rich and varied wildlife, are planned for logging and perhaps mining. The canyon forests of Noisy and Diobsud Creeks are scheduled for clearcuts that would deeply invade a remote alpine region essential to guarding the wildland integrity of North Cascades National Park.

North of the Nooksack River lies the Tomyhoi-Silesia area, one of the state's supreme terrains for high-country rambling, on and off trails, from the emerald meadows of Church Mountain east through tundra ridges and cirque lakes to Yellow Aster Butte, past the startling crags of the Border Peaks to Hannegan Pass, a major entry to the North Cascades National Park. Views from the Nooksack Crest extend to the Picket Range and peaks of Redoubt, Bear, and Spickard, to the San Juan

Islands, to the British Columbia Coast Range. Especially, though, in the pink of dawn and the rose of sunset and all through the the day, eyes are trained across the deep gulf of the Nooksack valley to watch the Watcher.

NORTH CASCADES NATIONAL PARK

In 1964, when The Mountaineers published Tom Miller's *The North Cascades*, revealing to a widely unsuspecting nation an area containing more than triple the amount of glacier ice in all the rest of the United States outside of Alaska, pundits were pronouncing "the national park movement is dead." The U.S. Forest Service, repeating old tactics, was doing its best to make it so by flourishing offers for an "Eldorado Peaks Area" that would give a status as vague and illusory as the "Mount Baker Parks Division" of the 1920s.

In 1968 the pundits were proven wrong by a victory that not only preserved a magnificence of rock and ice and forests and meadows and wildlife, but breathed new vigor into the idea so prematurely declared defunct.

The victory was—as most are—flawed. Unlike the Olympic Park compromise, where opponents were allowed to dictate a maximum size, opponents of the North Cascades Park were permitted to draw the boundaries! Preservationists rejoice that now among the "nation's crown jewels" are the Picket Range and the peaks of the Eldorado area, Thunder Creek and the Stehekin valley, Cascade Pass and Whatcom Pass. They remain incredulous that the park failed to include even one of the three most spectacular features of the region—Glacier Peak, Mount Baker, and Lake Chelan.

The proposals in these pages would in part rectify the omissions of the past by establishing new wildernesses and augmenting old ones. As was the Olympic Park Act of 1938, the North Cascades Act of 1968 was not a triumphal conclusion, but a new beginning.

Overleaf - *Mount Baker and Coleman Glacier*

Mount Shuksan, North Cascades National Park

Image Lake, Glacier Peak Wilderness

Troublesome Creek, Glacier Peak Additions

GLACIER PEAK WILDERNESS

"The last wild volcano," it's been called, with no roads on any of the slopes or anywhere near. The view from Image Lake over the forested valley of the Suiattle River to the high ice reflected in the lake waters is as famous as any mountain scene in America. Hikers throng from across America to know the brilliance of the glaciers and richness of the forests, the profusion of the flowers and the assortment of rocks—banded gneiss and schist from the pre-volcano peaks, lavas and cinders and tuffs, beds of pumice deposited by the eruption of twelve thousand years ago that blew ash to Saskatchewan.

Bob Marshall, cofounder of The Wilderness Society, saw Glacier Peak as part of a larger whole. To define that whole, in the thirties he walked the valleys and climbed the ridges at a desperate pace—a killing pace—and failed to see his dreams through. Ultimately his proposals were revived by The Mountaineers and allies, and after eight years of unremitting pressure the U.S. Forest Service, in 1960, conceded a wilderness.

The Glacier Peak Wilderness is a national treasure, but a mere fragment of Bob Marshall's grand design. The North Cascades National Park went far toward the fulfillment. However, there are many contiguous wildlands that belong in the wilderness, especially the trail corridors through low-valley forests, the entryways. The opportunity remains to realize most, if not all, of the vision of the 1930s.

GLACIER PEAK COUNTRY

When conservationists were denied a proper Glacier Peak Wilderness in 1960 they turned to "the alternative strategy" and sought a North Cascades National Park centered on Glacier Peak, extending from Lake Chelan and Lake Wenatchee to Monte Cristo and Marblemount. In 1968, Congress created a park with the boundaries shifted northward, leaving the controversy unresolved.

The Glacier Peak country is the largest expanse of pristine mountains in the Northwest. However, despite timber values that are generally so low that logging could be considered only tree-mining, and despite a recreation use that has doubled or tripled or quadrupled every decade in the past half-century, less than half the roadless area is guaranteed. What Bob Marshall set out to do in the 1930s, and The Mountaineers in the 1950s, largely remains to be done.

To cite a few examples, completion of the masterpiece requires:
• On the northwest, the glacier-covered crags of Snowking and Buckindy; the forests of Buck and Downey Creeks where jungles make the summits of the Dome and Spire area challenges for the doughtiest wilderness mountaineer; the Middle Fork Cascade River, adjoining the North Cascades Park, draining from Kool-Aid Lake and the ice cataracts of Formidable, way points on the Ptarmigan Traverse, the classic high-alpine tour of the nation.
• On the southwest, from the Monte Cristo area, with some of the most popular trails in the state, to the solemn cirques of Glacier Basin, Gothic Basin, Lake Blanca, and Goat Lake; and to the roping-up places for ascents of Big Four Mountain, whose massive north face dominates the South Fork Stillaguamish valley, and of Sloan Peak, "the Matterhorn of the Cascades," and of Monte Cristo Peak and Wilman Spires and Gothic and Del Campo and Columbia and Goblin and other peaks of the busiest climbing area of the state.
• On the south, the Cascade Crest, where the Pacific Crest National Scenic Trail is the longest, gentlest meadow walk in the Cascade Range; the flower fields of Poet Ridge; the paths of the Chiwawa and White Rivers, and the approaches to Glacier Peak.
• On the east, the rolling plateau of the Mad River drainage; the rounded ridges and open

Lake Blanca, Glacier Peak Additions

pine forests of the Entiat, where Washington merges into Wyoming and the Old West.

These additions would round out Glacier Peak Wilderness to its full "natural" size, encompassing ecosystems from nearly rain forest on the west to nearly desert on the east, and offer winter and summer range for the golden eagle and the mountain goat, the spotted owl and the moose, the bat and the mouse, the man and the woman, the young and the old.

Boulder River
Boulder Falls

HIGGINS MOUNTAIN

Bounded on the west by lowlands, cut off from the main Cascades on the north, east, and south by broad, deep valleys, is an island of mountains. Most have been clearcut to the summits, the onetime trail system virtually obliterated by roads, the few remnants abandoned to become impassable tangles.

Frost-edged leaves,
Higgins Mountain Area

58

One isle of wildness has survived. Tourists driving the North Fork Stillaguamish River highway stop to photograph the great sweep of Higgins Mountain from valley pastures to rugged summit. The distinctive feature of the peak is its dramatically exposed geologic structure, especially the enormous dip-slope slabs of the sedimentary strata that appear smooth enough for skateboarding.

The commercial value of the bits of remaining forest is low; the aesthetic values are too high to price. In the future, with the wilderness guaranteed and the trails rebuilt, Higgins will be famed among hikers for the Swisslike views from alpine meadows down to floodplain farms and across the wide gulf of the Stillaguamish to the hanging glaciers of Whitehorse and the digit summits of Three Fingers.

BOULDER RIVER-MOUNT DICKERMAN-THREE FINGERS COUNTRY

When a Puget Sound family wants a walk through old-growth cedar and hemlock, Douglas fir and Sitka spruce, in a rain-forestlike greenery so moist and lush that to pause for a rest is to risk having moss grow over the boots and ferns from the ears, and wants a picnic by a bouldery river beneath waterfalls filming down a canyon wall—and wants all this within a short drive from home, on an easy trail open in depths of winter as well as heights of summer—Boulder River is the choice. So beloved is the trail that a decade ago when the U.S. Forest Service sought suggestions for roadless areas, this valley received more than any other in the Mount Baker National Forest.

This valley kept its trees while those all around were losing theirs thanks to a canyon that barred logging railroads and, later, trucks. When a road approach over the ridge was found, still the chainsaws held back, restrained by the dubious quality of the timber and the questionable stability of the soil. Nevertheless, wilderness status has been denied. Somewhere behind closed doors is a plan waiting to be bulldozed into reality.

The wilderness-of-now extends from the low valley to the high meadow of Goat Flat, where night views over the cities stress the closeness to civilization. It continues to the glaciers of Whitehorse, hanging 6,000 feet over valley farms, and the peaks of Three Fingers, their unmistakable profile familiar to every traveler of the northern Puget Basin, both mountains being climbers' favorites. To the east the wildland includes the forests of Perry Creek, the meadows of Deer Pass, the blueberry patches of Forgotten and Dickerman—the connections to Monte Cristo country. And flowing west to the Stillaguamish are the pure waters that have preserved the river's fisheries when threatened by logging siltation in other tributaries.

GUNN-BARING COUNTRY EAGLE ROCK

No group of mountains in the state has been more gaped at by more people than the peaks along the lower Skykomish River: Mount Index on the south and Gunn Peak and Mount Baring on the north. The first important international recognition of the nonvolcanic North Cascades came when Frank Smythe, a leading British explorer and photographer of the Himalaya and many other ranges, drove the Stevens Pass Highway and included Gunn and neighbors in the same book with Snowdonia, the Cuillin Hills of Skye, the Matterhorn, and Everest.

From miles away the north face of Baring catches the eye—and chills the marrow of the climber who considers putting hands on it. No spot in the state more awes a hiker than Barclay Lake, where deep shadows brew up mists that feed the forest mosses, and where the view straight up the terrible wall brings to mind the childhood incantation, "Heavy heavy heavy hangs over thy head."

Only the merest scraps of valuable forests remain in the narrow and avalanche-swept valleys that cleave these rough and rocky peaks. Logging would demand the costly ingenuities of helicoptering and ballooning and skyhooking: technology of the timber-miner. The trees are best left as they are, for the looking.

59

Mountain tarn, Boulder River Area

Sunset over Eagle Rock Area

Barclay Lake, Eagle Rock Area

Moonrise over Gunn Peak, Eagle Rock Area

NASON RIDGE

In the era when tourists traveled mainly by train, the Great Northern Railway sought to entice traffic by advertising in Eastern newspapers: "Come to the Pacific Northwest and watch the forests burn." Few historians seriously suggest the company deliberately fostered the spectacles. Nevertheless, the rail route through Stevens Pass has been thoroughly denuded by a combination of fire and avalanche. The huckleberry picking is renowned. So is the fall-color show, when square miles of vine maple burst into flame.

The Nason Ridge Trail, some twenty miles along the crest from near Stevens Pass to Lake Wenatchee, is a glory of a sky walk, whether done in whole or part, climbing an access trail from forests and cirque lakes on the north, or from the vine maple on the south.

Commercial value is so close to zero that the only objection to wilderness designation has been from those who want no wilderness anywhere.

LAKE CHELAN - SAWTOOTH DIVIDE

The sinuous fifty-mile lane of Lake Chelan divides grassy savannas of the south from mountain forests of the north, ice-chiseled horns and arêtes of the west from ice-scalloped ridges of the east. The lake also brings together semidesert and glacial torrent, the harsh north and gentle south, rainy west and sunny east.

The Lakeshore Trail from Prince Creek to Stehekin has become a mythic springtime hike, best done in the weeks before the goats have followed the fresh growth of their favorite salads up the slopes and the rattlers have come out to warm their cold blood on the rocks; while the prairie star and balsamroot and blue-eyed Mary and chocolate lily and death camas are in bloom.

The Summit Trail from Navarre Basin to Stehekin long has been famed as one of the supreme easy-wandering ridge walks (or in winter, ski tours) in the nation. Meadow basins are the more dreamlike for the stark gneiss of the Sawtooths—Oval, Star, and Courtney Peaks—which belie their seeming menace by permitting easy scrambles to the summits. The high views reach west across the Chelan trough (seen as a blue haze of empty air) to the white giants of the Cascade Crest, and east across another gulf—the Methow Valley—to tawny, round hills.

Denied protected status by the U.S. Forest Service, part of the area has been handed over to systematic destruction by motorcycles. Logging trucks plan to move up Buttermilk Creek, War Creek, and other tributaries of the Twisp and Methow Rivers. Once there they will mine the big ponderosa pine and Douglas fir, which are too scattered and few to be of economic consequence, yet are numerous enough to keep the hiker on trails to the highlands gasping with admiration.

Chelan Mountains from Prince Creek,
Lake Chelan-Sawtooth Area and Glacier Peak Additions

62

Nason Ridge

Silver Star Peak

PASAYTEN WILDERNESS

Here are the largest meadowlands in Washington, the longest summer, the bluest sky. Here, too, because of the distance from major population centers, the dimensions of the wilderness, and the connection via Canadian wildlands to other mountain ranges, lives the wildest of the wildlife. It's grizzly country, even today. And *wolf* country.

The landscape is transitional in mood from the Alps to the Arctic. In the west the topography reflects the intense alpine glaciation typical of the near-ocean Cascades. In the east, however, the country dominantly was shaped by the continental glaciation that overrode all but a few high peaks, rounding the ridges and smoothing the vast tundras. Two subsequent alpine glaciations have scooped cirques and dumped moraines, but have modified the handiwork of the great ice sheet in only a minor way.

The Boundary Trail that extends from the eastern limit of the Cascades westward across the wilderness has become, in a very few years, almost as nationally famous as the Pacific Crest Trail to which it connects. The hiker who ascends from Iron Gate to Sunny Pass and gazes out over the sprawl of Horseshoe Basin may think he has strayed to the north slope of Alaska's Brooks Range. Contouring Bauerman Ridge he may wonder if he has somehow wandered to the Middle Sierra—and at Cathedral Lakes, to the High Sierra. Perhaps purely because of the name he may decide to spend a night on Bald Mountain, watching the Aurora Borealis dance across the northern sky and listening to the coyotes chorusing all around.

PASAYTEN COUNTRY

Few highways in the nation offer alpine scenery comparable to that along the North Cascades Highway as it climbs Early Winters Creek to Washington Pass, passing under the spectacular walls and crags of Silver Star, Kangaroo Ridge, Liberty Bell, and Early Winters Spires. Few mountain roads in the state are as popular as that from the Methow Valley to Harts Pass, with views to The Needles, Golden Horn, Tower, Azurite, and Ballard. No stretch of the Pacific Crest Trail is more scenic than that from Harts Pass over Grasshopper Pass and Methow Pass to the Snowy Lakes and Cutthroat Mountain and Rainy Pass, the path traversing cliffs and rockslides and creek gravels of the Golden Horn granodiorite where feldspar gives the rock—and the landscape—a distinctive rosy hue.

Yet none of this big country has the protection of park, or wilderness, or any other status not subject to the whims of the U.S. Forest Service. Among its current whims are plans to intensify timber-mining, which would eliminate all but scraps of old-growth forests in the valleys, and to finish off the huge and ancient ponderosa pine and even begin clear-cutting lodgepole pine, never before in Washington considered a commercial species. Scores of miles of new roads are planned, hun-

Little Tiffany Lake from Tiffany Mountain

dreds of miles of motorcycle runways, combining with the logging to reduce drastically the winter range of big game and the year-round range of nongame animals and birds.

In the hinterland of the Pasayten Wilderness and contiguous with it are other wildlands that demand to be preserved: Long Draw and Long Swamp, the forest-and-meadow approaches to Horseshoe Basin; the pristine valleys of Farewell Creek and Disaster Creek; the untouched Chewack River, including the high plateau of Twentymile and Thirtymile Creeks; and the Lost River, canyon entry to what is known locally as "the *wilderness* wilderness."

The job begun by the U.S. Forest Service in 1935 and continued by Congress in 1968, remains to be completed now, before the bulldozers and chainsaws move in.

PASAYTEN NEIGHBORS: TIFFANY MOUNTAIN, BEAVER MEADOWS, AND CHOPAKA MOUNTAIN

Along the eastern extremity of the North Cascades lie three wildlands, close neighbors of the Pasayten Wilderness, where protection is needed to preserve a full spectrum of the range's primeval wildlife habitats and plant communities.

The trail up Tiffany Mountain climbs gently from larch groves and meadow ponds to an island of lichen-covered rocks and alpine flowers on the 8,242-foot summit standing high above the forest green.

Ridgetop trails give long views over the Okanogan Valley and wind through forests broken by the delightful surprises of the Beaver Meadows.

The fault scarp of Chopaka Mountain plummets a rocky-rugged 6,700 feet—one of the great precipices of the nation—to a mile-wide valley bottom that was gouged out by a tongue of the continental glacier, once was filled by a glacial lake, and now is meandered by the Similkameen River. The scarp, managed by the federal Bureau of Land Management, has superlative scenic and ecological significance in itself and provides a refuge for both mountain goats and mountain sheep. It has further importance as a complement to the ice-smoothed summit mesa of Chopaka, much of which is guarded from the hooves of cattle by a wide felsenmeer ("rock sea") and therefore retains a pristine tundra where willow trees grow one inch high. Managed by the Washington Department of Natural Resources, the summit area is proposed for a state wilderness that would connect the Pasayten Wilderness to the scarp wilderness, giving the easternmost reach of the Cascades a wilderness finale unmatched by any mountain range on the continent and as aesthetically necessary as the chorale movement of Beethoven's Ninth Symphony.

Tiffany Lake

66

MOB SCENES

One thing it's hard to be in wilderness is lonesome. Even a person with a frequent craving for solitude, and much encouragement by family and friends to indulge the taste, finds plenty of company. I don't mean just mosquitoes, or those voices of a crazy-raving storm that set a philosopher pondering whether the world was created by a Friend or an Enemy. When the sun goes down and I'm alone, some old sense tells me I'm surrounded by trees and rocks and creeks who—not *which*—are trying to decide if I'm one of them, and if not. . .

Even in broad daylight a person can understand what ecologists mean when they say there is no empty space in nature, that a wildland is like the tea party Alice barged in on, the March Hare and Hatter and Dormouse crying, "No room! No room!" Alice snorted, "There's *plenty* of room!" and plunked herself down and the party went on. But was it the same party?

In June of 1946 I was the first person of the year—first *human* person—up the East Fork Dosewallips River. At a mineral spring I walked into a band of elk slurping the muck, and they ambled up the hill, which I appreciated, because they are a lot of creature to argue with. I continued along the trail under a jutting rock, felt eyes boring into the top of my head, looked up—and there they were, elk eyes very close to mine.

The meeting put me to noticing how many footprints were in the trail. Little feet, big feet, none wearing boots. After supper at Camp Marion I stoked the fire to push back the circle of darkness, and the flames cast long tree shadows out to join the dance of the ghoulies and ghosties and long-leggety beasties that went bump bump bump all through the night.

In the morning I proceeded up the valley, into snow, following the tracks of a very sizable population, some members quite weighty, judging by how the path was pounded to a trench. A mite nervy from lack of sleep, and having the elk in mind, I wondered who carried that much weight.

Rounding a grove of trees I learned who. Shambling down the snow trench was a shaggy black beast who outweighed me by a factor of several. I ceased shambling up the snow trench. The beast kept on, head hanging low, as if sleepy, maybe from a night as bad as I'd had, or even a whole winter. As delicately as I could I cleared my throat. The beast stopped, raised a massive head, and rolled two enormous eyes around the landscape, searching for me. And finding me. At a distance of a couple dozen steps, or perhaps half that many on a dead run, we stood staring. Any threats I might have made would have been idle, and the occasion didn't seem to call for small talk. Finally the beast shrugged and slobbered a little, evidently not in fear but disgust, and shambled off into the trees.

I met two more bears coming down the trail, a population density that rather plainly said, "No room! No room!" However, the question arose as to how many other bears might be coming *up* the trail, so I kept on.

A patch of heather on a knoll was melted out and in the middle a hen grouse was clucking and fluffing, inviting me to attack her. I was so pleased to meet a creature smaller than me that I graciously assured her I not only wouldn't attack her but would make a wide detour around her brood of chicks hiding in the heather.

Talk about ingratitude. I took a couple of steps—in the wrong direction, obviously—and

Grouse

the crazy mother was climbing my body and beating wings on my chest and yelling her head off.

I'd never had to fight a bird before and was badly shaken when I got to Dose Meadows, knowing my escape to civilization must run this gauntlet. To delay a while I plugged steps in soft snow to Lost Pass, crawled out on a rock, looked across the headwaters of the Lost River to Lost Ridge, and thought back to another mob scene.

• • •

We were a mob in ourselves, a gang of Scouts eating lunch at Three Sons Camp in the summer of 1940. The other mob was composed of the grouse hen trying to decoy us from her chicks, the deer peering curiously from the meadow, the marmots whistling from boulders—more animals all at once than most of us ever had seen outside a zoo.

Somebody yelled, "Elk!" Above, on the slopes of Lost Ridge, a band of fifty or sixty was grazing—more mass of animal than any of us ever had seen outside a cow pasture.

Somebody cried, "Bear!" Higher up the ridge a big black fur ball was shambling along.

Then, "Wolves!" On the crest, loping purposefully, were two definite canines.

Most likely that was my first meeting with coyotes, and if so I cherish the memory. Since then I've gotten to know them well, and sometimes have the notion that if I whistled and yelled, "Come, Shep!" one would cut loose from the pack and run up to me wagging its rear end. Understanding how the canine and the human got together, twelve thousand-odd years ago, is easy. How many of God's creatures truly like others of God's creatures in a nongustatory way?

But *were* they coyotes? At trip's end we

Blacktail deer

Black bear

Mountain goats

crossed paths with a pair of old hillwalkers who'd chanced to be just over the ridge the day of our sighting and had met the canines nose to nose. These old hillwalkers knew coyotes like brothers. They swore these were something else...

The Olympic wolf evolved into a distinct subspecies during the eons it was isolated by the Pleistocene glaciers. It lived on the Peninsula when my Uncle Bill did, early in the century. He used to entertain my kids by chasing them around his house, wearing a wolf skin. The wolf was still in the Olympics in the 1920s and many a pioneer's proudest moment was posing for the camera with gun and trophy.

The experts aren't sure when the end came.

On that July day in 1940 I may have been among the last of my species to see the last of another species—the last Olympic wolves in the history of the planet. Evidently in this case Alice came to the party and there *wasn't* enough room.

70

CLOSE ENCOUNTERS

A person who wants to see animals does best to go to the zoo, where they've no place to dodge when they see you first. I've never in my life laid eyes on a wild cat of any sort. I *have* followed minutes-old cougar tracks through fresh snow, and what added interest to the situation was having once been told by a fellow how he was following a cougar in the snow, turned back to camp, and found tracks going both ways—the cat had circled around and had been following *him*. Well, they say the only cougar that attacks a human is one that's too old and feeble and toothless to catch and chew a rabbit. Of course, you never know when you might run across an old and feeble and toothless cougar hungry enough to try to gum your ankle.

The seeing is only a small part of the excitement. The true thrill is knowing they are *there*, that you are in their home. For every eyeball encounter a hiker comes on scores of evidences of presences. Walking. Eating. Hunting for something to eat. Fleeing something that wants to eat it. A person who finds a porcupine's tail amid a mass-trampling of coyote tracks can reconstruct *that* battle to the death. A litter of bloody feathers tells the full story of an unwary bird struck down in midflight by a diving raptor, ripped apart with talon and beak. A neat little stack of hay drying in a meadow in September speaks of a pika's winter, snug in a rock cranny.

The seeing, when you're that lucky, is the frosting on the cake. The day we explored Whistler Basin and Ashnola Mountain and the head of Timber Wolf Creek—one of the largest expanses of tundra in the state—the north wind was whipping the grass in waves and hawks were sailing, never a flap, over the dips and rolls, inches from the ground. Rock chucks (Columbian ground

squirrels) were everywhere—standing on hind legs on their front porches, whistling warnings back and forth, so marmotlike we thought that's what they were. We'd be taking pictures of a chuck and wings would zip past our ankles and the chuck would dive into its hole. We never saw a kill and weren't anxious to. We weren't cheering for either side. Everybody's got a right to live but everybody's got to make a living, too.

I'm not sure to what extent *our* living requires the eating of wild animals. They generally have considerably more to offer us than a piece of meat. I'm positive we've got to stop mounting trophies on the wall of the war room. A few dozen pioneers had the satisfaction of shooting Olympic wolves and so the couple of million people a year who visit Olympic National Park have a zero chance to see one. I'd settle for a song.

As for people who'd shoot a mountain goat, presumably they'd also, given the opportunity, assassinate an elephant or a whale. Killing the creature that is the spirit of the high and wild is on the same order as clear-cutting the Hoh rain forest or open-pit mining Miners Ridge. Last summer we walked into a band of fifty-four goats at Cold Lake and watched them amble up snowfields and moraines and saunter across cliffs that would give a steeplejack the vertigo, the kids frolicking as if on a picnic. After a few hours we remembered we'd completely forgotten to climb Moon Mountain.

Periodically there's a crusade to get rid of the bears because they're ruining the national parks. With all due sympathy for the victims, the possibility of *being* a victim is what gives bear country a special flavor. Eliminate bears—and bear stories—and I doubt it would be possible to hold a decent campfire.

The first thing a hiker learns, of course, is that those aren't Teddy bears out there.

Hoary marmot

Squirrel

It's plain enough that no matter how fond a bear becomes of what people put in garbage cans and picnic baskets and packs, he never extends the sentiments to people. *Ursus* is always grumpy around *Homo*. With so many hikers nowadays, that means it's often a sour life, being a bear, especially a national park bear. When my two oldest girls were six and seven the three of us went camping at Rainier. They were up at dawn razzing around the woods while I slept. They ran out of razz and woke me up to entertain them. Told them to go away and play games. Came back and said they'd played all their games. Told them to go away and chase a bear. Heard laughing and screeching and they came on the run, yelling, "Daddy!

Daddy! We did what you told us and the bear ran up a tree and now he's *growling* at us!" So I got up.

I have a lot of empathy for bears, having been one once myself. I'd spent a few days up Thunder Creek and Skagit Queen Creek, making the year's first tracks—people tracks—in the snow. What gave the trip a peculiar suspense was that the previous fall a ranger had sighted two grizzlies thereabouts. I had a certain amount of curiosity about what would happen if we met, but we didn't, and I was sorry to miss out on a new bear story, but not *too* sorry. Hiking back to Colonial Creek Campground I rounded a bend in the trail and came on a family studying flowers. Well, I admit I'd grown careless about combing my hair and washing my face and sewing up rips in my britches, and maybe was still carrying on a quiet conversation with myself. So, mommy and daddy were showing a rattlesnake plantain to the kids when the littlest, a girl three or four years old, spotted me and let out a shriek that curled my toes. Over the years I've had a good many adverse reactions from females but never anything to touch *that*. She was in daddy's arms wailing and sobbing and I was wondering if it was time to buy a new shirt or trim my whiskers.

Daddy explained to me that they'd been at the campfire program and the ranger had told them how to identify bears: if you climb a tree and the bear climbs after you, that's a black, and if he stays on the ground and shakes you out of the tree, that's a grizzly. The little girl listened with eyes big as saucers and hadn't wanted to go on this flower walk at all and was keeping a sharp lookout for bad news. She spotted me and figured I fit the description.

I feel sad to this day, knowing a girl grew up with nightmares about me. Imagine how it must be for a *real* bear.

By and large I've always gotten along fairly well with bears. My nightmares are about *small* beasts. In the middle of the night at Norwegian Memorial a rustling woke me and I turned on the flashlight—and ten inches from my nose a spotted skunk was dragging away our bag of granola. It was extremely nervous, and when a skunk is nervous so is the whole neighborhood. But that granola was breakfast for the week. I took a polite grip on one end of the bag and the skunk tugged, and tugged, and got nervouser and nervouser, and me too. Then it let go of the bag and went into a dance and so did my heart. Finally it danced off in the dark. Ever since then if a mouse tiptoes by my sleeping bag I wake up sweating.

The skunk and I didn't dislike each other, we just had a policy disagreement. It was another matter with the Douglas squirrel at Scott Creek.

We were waiting out a stormy spell, holed up in the shelter. It's a popular spot, heavy backpacker traffic year-round, and that squirrel had gotten spoiled rotten. No puffed rice for him, or pilot crackers, or even peanut butter or cashews. He had a purely sweet tooth, and not for Hershey's bars or Nestlés. He was strictly a Cadbury squirrel.

At first we tossed pine cones his way to introduce the general idea of respect for private property. As the afternoon wore on any resemblance to a Disney animal wore off and we threw harder, aiming to thump his ribs. My boy, who also is partial to Cadbury, confessed he wouldn't mind giving the beast a bruise or even a mild concussion.

At night we stowed the Cadburys inside three layers of poly bag, inside a pack pocket zipped tight, and hung the pack—all the packs—from the rafters. Come morning we found the rascal either had been spying from his hideout or could sniff Cadburys through five layers of aluminum foil, poly, and pack cloth. He'd wasted no time prospecting, had leapt from the rafters to exactly the correct pocket of the correct pack and chewed a hole.

It was slow work, hanging upside down, and he'd only just broken through to the foil. Well, he was worn out from a sleepless night and crazy for a Cadbury fix. He'd dart in from the forest or out of a wall, jump off the roof, sail from a tree like a flying squirrel. We escalated our weaponry to rocks. Whenever we scored a solid hit he'd stagger off in the brush and groan awhile, then limp back to the attack.

That night we put the Cadburys in a cooking pot with the lid on tight and rocks piled on top. We lay in our bunks listening to the skitter of squirrel feet as he backed up to one end of the kitchen table to get a run and made a dash and banged his head on the pot. All night long. Skitter-bang, skitter-bang.

The Cadburys survived. In the morning we saw his opinion of us, written in squirrel scat all over the table. I can only say, the feeling was mutual.

The Eastern Corners

Aspens in the Okanogan Highlands

Forget-me-nots in the Kettle Range

Columbian ground squirrel,
Okanogan Highlands

Overleaf - Sand dunes in the Juniper Forest

OKANOGAN HIGHLANDS

East of the North Cascades, beyond the Okanogan Valley, rises another mountain range—better described as a hill country of modest elevation and subdued contours. The ecosystems, more continental than coastal, more "Montana" than "Washington," give a wilderness experience a world away from the western part of the state. Here there are *two* timberlines, the forest zone being bounded below by semidesert sagebrush steppe and above—on the highest peaks only—by subalpine gardens. Because of the variety of seed sources, the microsystems in nooks and crannies support surprising mixtures of plants.

Four substantial areas of the Okanogan Highlands remain roadless:
• Jackson Creek, draining to the Kettle River in Canada, has more rainfall than most parts of Eastern Washington. This area supports a more diverse vegetation, as well as a large population of deer.
• Mount Bonaparte, at 7,258 feet the highest summit, is extremely popular with hikers and horse riders and hunters who follow trails along the high ridges that are thinly forested with lodgepole pine and western larch. Wildland streams water the farms on the semidesert lands below.
• Clackamas Mountain feeds the Kettle and Sanpoil Rivers, which are important as fish habitat and for irrigation. The broken terrain provides solitude for the hiker, refuge for the wildlife.
• Dugout, a combination of rough cliffs and gentle meadows, is both a home and a migration route for a variety of large and small animals.

KETTLE RANGE

The Kettle Range is a place between, geologically and ecologically distinct from both the Cascades and the Rockies. Western Washington hikers come to study the unusual plant communities here, a transitional mixture of species. Eastern Washington hikers come because this is the largest remaining wilderness in a portion of the state that has very little left.

The Kettle Crest forests—beautiful to walk through and invaluable for wildlife habitat and watershed protection—are commercially important only in the way the placer gold of California was. The ponderosa pine grows to majestic size, but ever so slowly. Timber sales planned in the highlands by the U.S. Forest Service would give short-term prosperity to local mills, which then would fade away as permanently as Poker Flat because the next harvest would be centuries in the future.

Four areas that are still roadless—Thirteen Mile, Profanity, Bald-Snow, and Twin Sisters—are proposed for wilderness. The rolling ridges, the open forests, the parkland meadows and rocky balds on slopes of peaks 6,000 and 7,000 feet high offer superb hiking, as well as cross-country skiing following the snow tracks of wolverine and badger and marten, cougar and bobcat and lynx. The peaks catch clouds to make rain that is held in the soils of the wildland, a natural reservoir that serves arid lowlands by slowly releasing pure water for people and fish.

It is told that of old the Indian youths came here on vision quests. The hiker of today occasionally chances on lichen-covered rock cairns that tell of these long-ago searches for wisdom and enlightenment.

SALMO-PRIEST COUNTRY

An arm of the Selkirk Mountains that pushes over the border from Canada into Washington and Idaho forms the home hills for Spokane-area hikers. They are fond, indeed, of the groves of rain-forest red cedar up to twelve feet in diameter and 2,800 years in age, among the largest and oldest known to exist inland; of the meadow bogs bright with blooms of kalmia and Labrador tea; and of the arctic-alpine gardens on Gypsy Peak, at 7,309 feet Washington's highest elevation east of the Cascades.

The region's highest elevation, in Idaho, is Snowy Top at 7,572 feet, on the divide between the Salmo River and the Upper Priest River. The lowest, a valley at 2,720 feet, is on the Upper Priest, principal spawning stream of northern Idaho's Dolly Varden trout and listed by the National Scenic River Act as one of America's thirty-seven most scenic wild rivers.

Mountain Caribou
in the Salmo-Priest Area

Juniper cluster in the Juniper Forest

78

Sand dock in the Juniper Forest

These are important matters. However, from the standpoint of the nation—and the biosphere of Earth—the particular significance of the Salmo-Priest country is the unique wild-life community. There are Rocky Mountain bighorn sheep, moose, grizzly, and reportedly the gray wolf. Certainly there is a small band of mountain caribou, the only naturally resident caribou remaining in the lower forty-eight states and officially listed as an endangered species. It is sure to become an ex-species if it loses a crucial portion of its diet, the mosses and lichens occurring only in climax coniferous forests.

The U.S. Forest Service gives lip service to protecting the animals, yet plans timber sales wholly within irreplaceable grizzly and caribou habitat. The logging and roading would send the species on the run—species that have just about run out of places to run to.

JUNIPER FOREST

For thousands of years, since the time of the glaciers, the prevailing winds have been blowing grains of sand northeasterly from the Columbia River, building dunes that advance slowly across the plateau in classic marching formation. Over those eons a distinctive ecosystem has evolved, including one of the few remaining large examples of sandhill communities and sage-steppe grasslands in Washington. The northernmost stand of western juniper in North America is found here, and is of unique scientific importance because this *is* its extreme reach. Also over the eons the desert wilderness has become home to numerous species of arid-land wildlife, including four rare in the state—the ferruginous hawk, Ord's kangaroo rat, long-billed curlew, and pygmy rabbit—and the state's only group of scaled quail.

In the 1960s a scattering of motorcycles arrived, scouting. In the 1970s the main force of off-road vehicles—the ORVs—invaded in gangs, cutting fences erected for protection, eroding the sand hills, destroying plants, driving out birds and beasts.

The Juniper Forest cannot survive another such decade. The winds may repair the symmetry of the dunes in a few years. Not for centuries, possibly eons, could the plant communities and wildlife be restored.

The federal Bureau of Land Management, aware of this, nevertheless has deemed the ORV the most important species, has declared the highest use of the Juniper Forest to be a sandbox.

WENAHA-TUCANNON COUNTRY

A large wildland straddling the Washington-Oregon border contains the rugged east front of the Blue Mountains (the last remaining roadless refuge for the famous Blue Mountain elk herd) and the deep, steep canyons of the upper Tucannon River and of the entire Wenaha River from headwaters to its junction with the Grande Ronde River. The waters, seeming the brighter and colder for the hot summer sun on grassy-shrubby canyon walls, support whitefish, rainbow trout, and Dolly Varden trout year-round, and provide spawning grounds for salmon and steelhead. Ridges sprawl in all directions, spottily forested by ponderosa pine, lodgepole pine, western larch, and white fir. A profusion of lesser canyons, in which many of the creeks are intermittent, carve the country into sublimely rough scenery. Secure from the intrusion of the internal-combustion engine, it's a lonesome land: refuge for the elk, deer, bear, cougar, bald eagle, and golden eagle, and for the fisherman and hiker in three seasons, the horse-riding hunter in one, and in another, the cross-country skier and snowshoer.

continued heavy and sweaty, electrical. Their night at Stehekin the families were deafened and drenched, and again the next night at Grizzly Creek. The afternoon of August 12, arriving in North Fork Meadows, at 3,800 feet beneath the north wall of 9,200-foot Goode, the party took note of the funny-looking clouds—funny in a way that doesn't make mountaineers smile.

There being no trees at Many Waterfalls Camp, which was set in the tall grass of the alluvial fan of a North Fork tributary, tarps were rigged from bipods of dead limbs brought down by avalanches. The tributary being dry, the kitchen was established in its gravel bed. The fire was built, soup pots were hung from dinglesticks, and the storm broke.

By the standards of that summer it was a moderate squall and soon moved east toward the peak of McGregor. The families crawled out to drink soup. One camper, eyeing the funny sky above Logan, to the west at the valley head, remarked, "Somehow I doubt we've heard the whole story."

At eight o'clock he bent down to hang pots of water on the dinglesticks to boil for the main-course hoosh, stood—and was transfixed. Rolling over the summit ridge of Logan with the look of a swollen river topping a dike, was such a cloud as he'd never seen, of an evil, yellow-red hue, burning with such a violence of fires as he'd never seen. By reflex he began the count and reached ten before the thunder cracked—two miles, the distance to Logan.

Once begun the thunder never stopped. The cloud turned a dense gray lit by inner furnaces and flowed waterfall-swift down the face of Logan. The count shortened to eight, to six, to four. The families dived under tarps and crawled into bags, as if a few ounces of goose down and nylon might stave off Armageddon.

The cloud filled the valley from side to side; the solid front advanced faster than a person could sprint, extinguished the shrub-topped knoll above camp, hurricaned the tall grass, bellied out the tarps like sails of a clipper ship rounding the Horn, and pounded the sleeping bags with hail.

Thunder was simultaneous with lightning that was blinding *inside* bags drawn over heads and *under* lids closed over eyes. A ten-year-old girl screamed, "We're all going to die!" Her father silently agreed, and wondered if what he was feeling was in fact the sensation of being electrocuted.

The hail passed quickly on, and the wind too—luckily, since the tarp guys were pulling loose. Rain as heavy as a giant's hand pressed tarps down on bags and held them there.

The storm flamed continuously in a dozen places at once—cloud-to-cloud discharges ten thousand feet above and a hundred feet above—cloud-to-ground strikes on all peaks and ridges of the North Fork—and, it was suspected, on tall trees in the forest—and, it was feared, potentially on bipod poles conspicuously above meadow grass.

A buttress tower of Goode burned in a white-hot current almost ceaselessly, until it seemed the rock must flow in red-hot lava down the mile-high wall. Fires other than lightning *were* burning on Goode—sparks hundreds of feet long, struck by the crash of rock on rock. The rumble of thousands of tons of falling mountain reinforced the thunder, and so did a steady, growing roar revealed by lightning to be the Many Waterfalls, swoollen to mud-brown Niagaras.

Numb minds dwelt not on life and death, philosophy and cosmology, only on the count between flash and bang. Not for two hours was any count possible—who could tell which thunder went with which lightning? Then three was reached, and five, and ten, and the cloudburst diminished to hard rain; the storm had become Mount McGregor's business, and the sleep of the

THE QUIETEST DAY

shell-shocked began—and at eleven o'clock ended as a second storm blazed on Logan. Two hours it raged over Many Waterfalls before moving toward McGregor. Then a third storm spilled over the crest. And another, and another, and as drained of fear as hope the campers awoke only at the dazzle-wham of each new arrival's first announcement.

At ten in the morning old thunder dwindled to a distant rumble and no new thunder crackled. The families emerged to sun and blue, followed the tributary, no longer dry, downstream to retrieve the kitchen, and gazed in awe at the Many Waterfalls, brown and enormous, shuddering the meadows. The Goode wall, so chaotic in the night, was solid and quiet as Gibraltar. The sky above Logan was serene. The grass waved gently in a refreshing cool breeze, flowers glowed in the sun, and on the knoll above camp an elk grazed. And so for the remaining three days the North Fork was good, true, and beautiful.

On the hike out the storm retroactively struck the party dumb with the ultimate terror. Several minutes down the trail an alluvial fan that had been the twin of the one they had camped on at Many Waterfalls was buried ten feet deep under boulders and gravel and smashed trees, the debris of a blowout flood.

Stehekin elders called the storm "the worst since 1912." Of the three girls in the party, the ten-year-old and eleven-year-old took pride ever after in having known the power of the wilderness as few hikers are privileged to do—and live. As for the four-year-old, through the years whenever the family exchanged memories of the Sixteen Hour Storm she grumbled. The youngest always gets cheated. She went right to sleep after the soup and missed the whole show.

Still waters of Benchmark Lake mirror spiketop subalpine firs and blue morning sky. Rays of the rising October sun pierce the forest to set meadow dew glittering.

The hikers set out from camp for a day's exploration of the parkland plateau—a mountain plateau but not *in* mountains. The trail winds through groves of trees ringing small meadows of yellowing grass and reddening huckleberry leaves—a series of framed miniatures, not foregrounds for spectacular high backgrounds but complete in themselves.

No rivers roar, near or far. No creeks gurgle—few flow at all, and they in silent meanders.

At Henry Lake the sun catches milling gnats and the trout leaping for them. Dragonflies hover heavily in midair and abruptly dart. The airship of a spider gone a-roving glints above the water, drifting in a convection breeze stirred by the warming day.

No other people are met or heard and the hikers speak low, communicating mainly with gestures and nods.

They linger to eat the low-bush Cascade huckleberry, *vaccinium deliciosum*, and the high-bush and even more delicious black huckleberry, varying the menu with the tart flavor explosions of the tiny red grouseberry. A few flowers continue in bloom, cinquefoil and paintbrush and bistort and aster in meadows, arnica among lichen-black stones of oozing creeks, phlox on rocky knolls. Grasshoppers hop high in clouds of lupine perfume.

Squeals of hawks and squawks of gray and Steller's jays are events so startling they break the rhythm of the boots.

A pond is splashed green and yellow with pads and blossoms of pond lily, polliwogs swim amid floating grass, and the shore is a woolly white field of lamb's lily in seed head.

At Big Twin Sisters Lake the breeze ripples the surface to a constellation of sparkles

Mount Adams from Goat Rocks Wilderness

yet never grows to a wind, scarcely sighs in the trees. A gull perches on a shore boulder. Somewhere something goes *ook ook*.

Forest floors are brightened with the garish orange and warty menace of amanita. A coral mushroom and a king boletus are picked to add to the evening meatballs and gravy.

The beach of Little Twin Sisters Lake forces off the boots, time for a wade in gentle waves. The hikers marvel at such a quantity of sand, wonder where it all came from...

The trail turns up Tumac Mountain, climbing hard lava ledges and loose cinders—red, pink, green, black, brown, yellow. A side path leads through trees to a crater with a snowfield and lakelet, water supply for the onetime fire lookout. Scooped from the mountainside below is a larger crater, also with a lake. The hikers are surprised to see this peaklet is not, as usually described, a cinder cone, a one-shot burping of gas and ash, but a composite volcano built over time by alternation of flows and blasts.

In late afternoon they reach the summit and gaze over the forest plateau, each tree delineated in the low sun and casting a long shadow. In limpid air the sharp-edged darkness of Tumac comes to a point far across the plateau. To north and east the rounded crests of Nelson Ridge and American Ridge, the splinters of Bismarck and Aix, the forests

of Bumping River, show crisp and clean in the play of light and dark. To west and south the smoke of loggers' slash-burning blurs ridges and valleys to landscapes on the boundary of dreams.

The hikers gaze at Rainier, a mature stratovolcano deeply dissected by glaciers largely composed of icefalls, except for the Emmons and Winthrop, whose broad white ramp fills the cavity blown out five thousand years ago by the steam explosion that sent the Osceola Mudflow bellowing down the White River to the saltchuck.

They turn to Adams, of matching bulk and only a half-mile less high, a companion in middle age.

And to Tieton and Old Snowy and Gilbert, skeleton of the long-dead Goat Rocks volcano, stripped to the bone.

And to graceful St. Helens, so youthful the slopes are barely gouged by ice, and said by vulcanologists in this year of 1976 to be uneasily dormant, in fact due for a major eruption, perhaps soon.

Ringed by volcanoes old and mature and young, the hikers stand atop an infant volcano that perhaps was the vent from which the lava flowed to fill the primeval valleys, creating this plateau. Remembering their geology, the hikers realize this was how Rainier began.

They gaze to the silent plateau. Silent *now*.

The Southern Cascades

GOAT ROCKS WILDERNESS

In 1931 the Goat Rocks Primitive Area was established, one of the first two Washington wildlands recognized by the U.S. Forest Service. A half-century later it is among the most popular hiking areas in the state, traversed by the Pacific Crest Trail, which attains a scenic climax in the colors of the rocks, roots of a volcano once on the scale of Mount Adams, and of the blossoms so richly nourished by lava-and-cinder soils and snowfield meltwater.

In the olden days "primitive areas" were laid out in a primitive manner, by drawing straight lines and right angles easy to place on primitive maps. Minor adjustments to the olden-day lines would provide logical, natural boundaries and would round out the wilderness by adding forest approaches in the Cispus, Cowlitz, and Tieton Rivers; Packwood Lake, in a deep valley beneath high ridges; and Bear Creek Mountain, a dream-wander garden culminating in a panorama of volcanic pinnacles and broad glaciers to the west, and forests thinning to sagebrush hills to the east.

Protection also could be extended to Conrad Meadows in the South Fork Tieton River, the largest valley-bottom subalpine meadow in the state, a Montanalike ecosystem not represented in any of Washington's preserves and thus of great scientific importance. Only in the summer of 1980, when St. Helens ash lay heavy and gray on the "Ghost Rocks," were hikers privileged to enjoy the glory of flowers. Ordinarily the cows eat them.

MOUNT ST. HELENS NATIONAL VOLCANIC MONUMENT

During the long years when conservationists sought a national monument to halt the plundering of the "Fuji of the West," they often joked about the chances of the volcano doing what Mount Lassen, farther south in the Cascades, had done to catch the attention of Congress and become a national park.

May 18, 1980, St. Helens did so, rendering moot many old arguments about roadless areas and opening new ones about the management of natural phenomena unmatched in the nation for their complexity and fascination. Conservationists reacted to the changed situation by striving not solely to save the forests from destruction, as they had before, but to save the scene of natural destruction from human destruction, to preserve a scientific museum and laboratory.

The volcano will, of course, take care of itself. The lava dome will continue to grow in the new crater—or perhaps blow itself to bits that will be deposited on Yakima, Tacoma, Portland, Seattle, or wherever. But the lava-tube caves, the longest known in the world, need proper care to preserve these fossilizations of old eruptions. It is necessary to prohibit logging in both the ancient forests that survived the blast and those that were leveled to matchsticks; to let the native plants—not introduced exotics—spread their pioneering green over the

Overleaf - *Mount St. Helens and the Goat Rocks Wilderness*

Goat Rocks Wilderness

brown and gray of mudflows and ash heaps; and to prevent overeager engineers from the unnecessary wielding of bulldozers.

Something of this will be done. Working at a pace unknown to it since Lassen erupted, in 1983 Congress established the national volcanic monument, under the U.S. Forest Service. The monument is not the 216,000 acres sought by preservationists but 110,000, and the protective regulations have weaknesses. The discussion must therefore continue, in the expectation that St. Helens may well have something more to say.

THE COUNTRY BETWEEN THE VOLCANOES: DARK DIVIDE AND TRAPPER CREEK

Until recent years, Gifford Pinchot National Forest was an enormous wilderness unity of forested ridges and valleys, a sea of green waves. Hikers and horsemen could follow trails from Rainier to the Columbia, St. Helens to Adams, and cross scarcely a road. A mere quarter-century has transformed the area to a

Pre-eruptive Mount St. Helens overlooking the Dark Divide

sea of clearcuts in which float a scattering of roadless islands.

These few remaining isles, with their low-elevation valleys and ridgetop vistas, are the last pristine remnants of a geographical and ecological province unlike any other in Washington. They must be preserved if the wilderness system is to be fully representative of the primeval Northwest.

The largest proposed preserve is the multi-lobed Dark Divide, containing the historic Boundary Trail, the virgin valley of Quartz Creek, and Blue Lake.

Farther south, Trapper Creek has the last unlogged valley so near the Columbia, traversed by a trail out of Government Mineral Springs that dates from the frontier.

This was the national forest chosen, from all those in the country, to serve as a memorial to Gifford Pinchot, the man who shaped the U.S. Forest Service and gave it the motto, "the greatest good of the greatest number in the long run." Nobody ever has understood exactly what that means. It is only clear that in a rather short run the wilderness is nearly gone in Pinchot country.

MOUNT ADAMS WILDERNESS

Had Adams instead of Rainier become a national park, Bird Creek Meadows would be as famous as Paradise, the Adams Glacier as the Nisqually, the Devils Garden as Yakima Park, the Round-the-Mountain Trail as the Wonderland Trail. One of the great volcanic peaks of the world, Adams made an unlucky (or lucky?) choice of neighborhood and became the "Forgotten Giant of Washington."

In 1942 the U.S. Forest Service showed decent respect by placing the mountain in a protected wildland—only the third in the state. However, as was customary in those days, the boundary was drawn without regard to the natural bent of the terrain or the integrity of ecosystems. Moreover, the purist policy of the time was to leave buffer zones around a wilderness so that when a person entered the preserve he was already beyond sight or sound of

machines. Unfortunately, the Forest Service that can't remember Leopold is proceeding to log the buffers.

To preserve the wholeness of the giant, the boundaries need to take in such features as the four-mile-long Aiken Lava Flow, Adam's most recent lava eruption, some one thousand years old; the Salt Creek-Cascade Creek valley, the only low-forest approach still wild; Stagman Ridge, the most scenic approach to the west side; and South Butte, a 7,800-foot parasite vent. Finally, the present wilderness omits—incredibly—much of the Pacific Crest Trail, world-famous even though Adams isn't, yet.

INDIAN HEAVEN

Near its southernmost Washington reach the Pacific Crest Trail traverses fourteen miles of subalpine forest and meadow liberally sprinkled with lakes, seven big enough to have names and a hundred or two smaller ponds and pools. The path follows a backbone of old volcanic vents—Red, Gifford, East Crater, Sawtooth—that stand high enough above the lava plateau to give long views to the glaciers of the great volcanoes sprawled along the range from Hood to Rainier.

September is the hiker's favorite month, the mosquitoes gone, the colors of the berry bushes turning, the fruit ripening. It also is the best season for feeling presences.

It is not known when people first climbed to these highlands. For centuries prior to the arrival of the Europeans, and perhaps eons, they had been coming to crop their berry "farm"—created by regularly setting fires to discourage encroaching forests. In later years, after obtaining the horse from the Spanish, they brought their cayuses for sport.

These must have been the happiest of times, the hard work of harvesting the fall salmon run over, the picking and drying of berries a sort of vacation. In chill autumn nights the folks sat close around the campfires, drinking huckleberry wine and betting on the next day's horse races. The harvest moon sparkled on frosted meadows. Old Coyote perched atop a volcano, singing.

Mount Adams Wilderness

Misty morning at Junction Lake, Indian Heaven

Sword ferns and thimbleberry in the Issaquah Alps

THE WILDNESS WITHIN

The twilight song begins in Klondike Swamp, joined by howls, moans, and yips from lava outcrops of De Leo Wall and pastures of The Pass, cattails of Long Marsh and waterfalls of the Far Country, cliffs of The Precipice and virgin forest of The Wilderness. Suburban dogs rage up and down patios, answering. City dogs carry the chorus south from Renton to Kent and Auburn and Tacoma, north from Bellevue to Kirkland and Bothell and Edmonds and Everett, west from Mercer Island to hills and valleys and beaches of Seattle. Atop Cougar Mountain, where he started it all, Old Coyote rests content.

Where he sometimes lives, in the Issaquah Alps, is not the classic wilderness. Cedar stumps notched for fallers' springboards, tumbledown bridges of logging railroads, cave holes where the earth has slumped into old mines, climbing roses and Deptford pink and periwinkle from gardens of vanished Red Town, tell of generations of living and trammeling. However, half a century ago, after the old-growth forests were hauled to the mills and cheap petroleum closed the coal mines, thousands of acres of Cougar, Squak, Grand, Taylor, and Tiger were abandoned. It's not the wilderness of Muir and Leopold and Marshall and Zahniser, but in an age when more people visit Everest base camp each year than, several decades ago, climbed Mount Si, what is?

Unless we make-believe. As we do in the Bailey Range and the Picket Range, Spray Park and La Bohn Gap, Elbow Basin and Shi Shi Beach; as we do because inside every civilized creature is a wild one remembering. That's why the dogs bark.

From earliest times, Puget Sound City has been known for a green soul, for a wealth of next-to-home nooks where the needing and believing can step directly from city street into jungles of the Amazon. Though the dismal science of megalopolitan economics devises a gray scheme for every green nook, Bellingham still has Chuckanut Mountain; Anacortes, Mount Erie and Heart Lake; Mt. Vernon-Sedro Woolley, Little, Devils, and Cultus Mountains and the Skagit marshes; Bremerton, the Green and Gold Mountains; Olympia, the Nisqually Delta and the Black Hills.

Even the dense core of Puget Sound City has many wild spots, from Everett's Howarth Park to Seattle's Discovery Park to Tacoma's Point Defiance Park, from Kirkland's St. Edward's Park to Bellevue's Bellefields Park to Auburn's Blue Heron Marsh to Black Diamond's Green River Gorge, and scores more.

The only *large* wildland *within*, however, is the long finger of the Old Mountains thrusting twenty-five miles from the Cascade front to Lake Washington: the Issaquah Alps.

It's not wilderness. Don't tell the wild animals, though, lest you spoil their dinner. A cougar regularly tours Cougar Mountain to levy a top-of-the-food-chain tax on the rabbits and deer. Elk browse amid the thousand-year-old Douglas firs of the Issaquah Watershed, inside the city limits, and graze sheep pastures of May Valley nearly to shores of Lake Washington. In summer the bears harvest Indian plums and blackberries; in late fall they top-prune apple orchards once tended by coal miners for the making of pies and the brewing of grapa. The great blue heron stalks the salmon that spawn from fall to spring in creeks that flow to Lake Sammamish and Lake Washington; the fish lure the bald eagle, a year-round resident. The water ouzel, John Muir's favorite, walks underwater, gripping the bottom stones of Issaquah Creek, a stone's throw from Issaquah City Hall.

And don't tell the civilized animals of the Alps it's not wilderness. Local chickens nourish the raccoon and opossum, red-tailed hawk, and great horned owl. Dogs know the claws of the bobcat and teeth of the fox, barbs of the porcupine and gas of the skunk. House cats have the haunted eyes of a species that knows it is edible.

On a summer night Old Coyote likes to lie out on the rocky summit of West Tiger Mountain amid the tiger lily and spring gold, oxeye daisy and blue lupine, Indian paintbrush and littleflower penstemon; gaze the length and breadth of the Puget Basin from the San Juan Islands to the Black Hills, Olympics to Cascades, and marvel at the brilliance of million-eyed Puget Sound City.

It's not the world of his youth, in the time of the glaciers, before the people came. Who'd have thought, when the first bands straggled in from the north, there ever would be so many? Yet this still is *home*, for him and the people, not all of whom think they *own* the land. On the whole he rather likes them. When they arrived a dozen eons ago, shivering in winter and thirsting in summer, he took pity on their plight and stole fire from the Volcanoes and water from the Frogs. For the ones who got here just a century ago and hardly know where they are, if only they'll heed his twilight song he'll help them become one with the land.

THROUGH SEVEN DOORS

The first door
Climb the slopes of Mount Rainier above
Paradise Valley nearly to Panorama Point,
glissade to the Nisqually Glacier, ascend the
Snow Finger and Wilson Glacier to The
Castle. Elevation gain, from 5,500 to 9,500
feet. Time, seven o'clock to noon. Left
below: big trees, big rivers, bears, and deer;
little trees, little creeks, squirrels, and chipmunks; grass, flowers, marmots, camp
robbers, ptarmigan. Also: machines, radios,
neon, asphalt, lodges, milkshakes. What's left:
raw mineral, naked energy. Sit and eat a big
lunch, luxuriating in hubris.

The second door
The pack has gained weight. Legs have lost
spring. Heart and lungs have gone out of
synch. Lunch lies lumpily in the gut. Breathe
deep. Rest often. At three o'clock, 11,500
feet, fall down at Camp Hazard, humble.

Lie despairing in ash and cinders at the
base of the Kautz Ice Cliff, at a camp higher
than any summit in the state save Adams
and The Mountain itself. Look down to the
colors of Earth: haze-blue forests in the
distance, moth-eaten by clearcuts; blue-green
parklands below; much brown all around in
cliffs; much white in glaciers; no flower to be
seen, nor bird to be heard; and there is too
much sky.

The wind nags, gusts threaten. The Ice
Cliff creaks and casts ice chunks down on
the ash, nearly to camp. The air is not the
air of Earth, it is an alien gas, the atmosphere of Mars.

The third door
Unroll the sleeping bag behind a boulder
windbreak that doesn't break the wind,
rather funnels blasts through crannies, yet
gives something more solid than sky to

Mount Rainier

Paradise meadow in Mount Rainier National Park

huddle against. Crawl in and wrap up in a bit of tarp and cover the head. Do not watch the sunset lest you lose your nerve and run barefoot and shrieking down the glaciers toward the lights of Paradise.

Hailstones rattle the tarp, thunder shudders the rocks under your body and the teeth in your skull. Do not look outside lest the lava cliffs be lit by ghastly torches of Saint Elmo's fire.

At four o'clock the night and wind are pierced by a wail summoning doomed souls. Crawl out, struggle into parka and boots, hold flashlight in teeth to lash on crampons, stand up and tie in to the rope, don mittens, shoulder rucksack, grasp ax, and join the line of fireflies sliding down the rubble gully beneath the Ice Cliff, rounding the lava nose to the Kautz Chute.

The fourth door
Crunch crampon spikes into the Chute's steep névé. Flashlights blink out. Dawnlight reveals a horizon-to-horizon cloudsea floating the island snowcones of Adams, St. Helens, Hood, Jefferson, and The Sisters, only these and nothing more.

Chop steps up ice gullies and seracs to where the upper Kautz Glacier gentles out at 12,000 feet. Climb faster, exalted by the Platonic simplification to dazzling whites of glacier and cloudsea, vibrant blue of sky. Stop, weary and sick. Sip grape juice, carefully, to settle the stomach and stiffen the legs. Ignore pastel snows along the route, where sips of orange juice were tried, and tomato juice and pineapple juice and chocolate milk. Resume the climb slower, a breath per step.

It is such strangely insubstantial air. Given such air as this no fish ever would have squirmed from the primordial soup and grown feet.

The fifth door
Step across hoarfrosted rocks of Wapowety Cleaver, 13,000 feet, from Kautz to Nisqually—not the Nisqually known below, a glacier flowing through rainbow meadows to green forests, but a glacier in the sky. Look back down toward the brink of the Chute, unseen, to waves of the cloudsea that has risen to submerge every isle but this Rainier. In

gray deeps lie Hazard, two doors below with sleeping bag and tarp, and Paradise, as drowned as Atlantis, with all its cameras and chipmunks and peanuts and rangers and hamburgers, five doors remote, too many. It is too late to turn back. The underworld is gone forever. Fate awaits above, at the rendezvous.
The sixth door
Breathing twice per step, round the end of the bergschrund of the Nisqually, a crevasse on the scale of The Mountain, off the human scale, blue-vasty depths shading downward to dreadful night.

Wake up. From a reverie—or a sleep? The pace of the feet is that of a dream, and so is the pace of the mind. Climbers have been known to fall asleep while walking, here, and continue upward, and meet Others crawling from crevasses.

Did you really wake up? Or only dream it?
The seventh door
At 14,000 feet, in the saddle between Point Success and Columbia Crest, pause for a sip of grape juice. Resume at three breaths per step.

It *was* a dream. Now it is a dream *within* the dream, and never can you find the route back through the labyrinthine subconscious to waking, through the maze of doors to Paradise, lost.

At ten o'clock four breaths and a step lift parka hood and goggles up into a gale from the Pole. Once more, and again, and crampons bite the crest and only these daggers stabbed into the outermost bulge of Earth prevent the wind from flinging the climber into space to collide with stars and bounce them around the galaxy like billiard balls.

A comrade—or an Other?—approaches, offering an open can of smoked oysters, and the grape juice fails and the initiation is complete.
And the door beyond
Later, in a place where flowers bloom and birds sing and butterflies flutter and the green grass grows all around, gaze to The Mountain and be proud to have stood in the middle of the sky, 14,416 feet tall.

In a soft summer night gaze to the Milky Way and be afraid to have been there—and glad to live on the good and green and pleasant Earth.

The Central Cascades

MOUNT RAINIER NATIONAL PARK

In the summer of 1896 a National Forest Commission sponsored by the National Academy of Sciences toured the West. On its recommendation, supported by mayors, chambers of commerce, newspapers, hotels, restaurants, philosophers, poets, the Northern Pacific Railroad, and Congress, in 1899 Rainier was inducted into the national park system, preceded only by the geysers of Yellowstone and

Overleaf - *Prusik Peak and pre-dawn light, Alpine Lakes Wilderness*

Below - *Mount Rainier from Summit Lake in the Clearwater River Area*

104

the canyon of Yosemite and the giant sequoia of the Sierra.

The bulk of The Mountain captures the eye and instills awe, yet is not the most distinctive characteristic. Rainier chances to lie precisely the appropriate distance between the North Pole and the equator, and in exactly the proper proximity to the ocean, to produce a climate with a temperature and moisture to please snowflakes and flowers alike. To the south in California the meadows are more, the glaciers less. To the north in British Columbia the glaciers are more, the meadows less. At Rainier they are in matching scale. Nowhere else in the world do ice so blind and color so enchant so simultaneously.

The names on the map summarize the human response: Sunrise Park, Sunset Park, Spray Park, Mist Park, Vernal Park, Grand Park, Emerald Ridge, Summerland, Elysian Fields, Paradise Valley. Through these and other wonders runs the Wonderland Trail.

MOUNT RAINIER: CLEARWATER RIVER AND GLACIER VIEW— TATOOSH

The pity is that when the entirety of Rainier's geologic and ecologic and aesthetic unity easily could have been set aside, the job was only done halfway. The historical record suggests a universal assumption: the grandeur of Rainier—Tahoma—The Mountain—would be sufficient defense. The assumption took too generous a view of human nature, the forest industry, and the U.S. Forest Service.

On every side—but most importantly on the north, in Clearwater country—the national park needs either to be enlarged or supplemented by wilderness: for the sake of the animals that spend part of the year in the park, part out; for the sake of human visitors who feel crowded in the park; and for the sake of The Mountain, which surely has established its right to have standing in the eyes of the law at least equal to any man, any corporation of man, any generation of men.

To complete what was only begun in 1899, Tahoma—Rainier—wants:
• On the north: The old-growth forests, alpine meadows, and cirque lakes at the head of the Clearwater River. Also, to enfold the upper Carbon River, Carbon Ridge—which is the lower frame for the view of Willis Wall from Seattle. These hiking meadows and fishing lakes are so near downtown Tacoma that they are used by the public schools for outdoor classrooms; a Tacoma-to-Tahoma Trail has been proposed from Commencement Bay up the Puyallup River and Carbon River to the glaciers. The photographs of Rainier taken from the vicinity of Summit Lake probably have been more often enlarged and hung on walls, and more often published, than from any area other than Paradise Valley.
• On the west: Puyallup Ridge, to preserve in trail country one of the most stunning vistas of The Mountain, from the site of a onetime fire lookout, Glacier View.
• On the south: The portions of the Tatoosh Range left out of the park, including Tatoosh Butte, locale of Martha Hardy's famous book, *Tatoosh*, and of Backbone Ridge and Lookout Ridge and the Muddy Fork of the Cowlitz River.
• On the east: The Cougar Lakes country, of course.

COUGAR LAKES— GREENWATER COUNTRY

A hiker on the Pacific Crest Trail may be immersed in ocean mists that lushly green up the meadow grass on House Mountain, above the Cougar Lakes, while another, several miles east, basks in sunshine amid flowery fell-fields atop Nelson Ridge. The raw cliffs and rough crags of Aix and Bismarck lie close by the lake-dotted parklands of Tumac Plateau, built of lava flows from infant stratovolcanoes. The huge old Douglas firs of the Greenwater River contain the distillation of centuries of rain. The huge old ponderosa pines of Rattlesnake Creek contain the essence of centuries of sun. Mountain goat scramble precipices of Fifes Peak. Native cutthroat swim the Rattlesnake—which also slakes the thirst of the people of Yakima.

Twin Lakes in the Clearwater River Area

Reeds on Twin Lakes

Tatoosh Range (Wahpenayo Peak)

Why, with all this to offer, has the Cougar Lakes–Greenwater country been denied permanent protection? Initially, the chief opponent was a politically powerful timber company that had no economic interest in the area but fought wilderness on knee-jerk principle. Then came a buzz of motorcycles to covet Indian Creek and a roar of jeepers the Little Naches and a snarl of snowmobilers the Tumac Plateau. Though plentiful nearby terrain is wide open to noise sports, the U.S. Forest Service took the interlopers as an excuse to hoist on high the begrimed banner of multiple-use, a cover for "liquidating the inventory" of old-growth timber in valleys and getting on with the next phase—mining the timber off the high ridges.

The history of Cougar Lakes during the past half-century: **1930s:** Constituting as it does the natural extension of Mount Rainier National Park, with contrasting and comple-

The Cougar Lakes

mentary topography and climate, and lacking significant economic value, the area is offered by the U.S. Forest Service to the National Park Service, which declines on the grounds the existing park is all it can handle. **1946:** Cougar Lakes is designated a Limited Area, defined by a Forest Service officer as meaning, "We haven't figured out where to put the logging roads." **1958:** They figure it out and sell timber on American Ridge. **1961:** In response, a proposal is written by Kay Kershaw and Isabelle Lynn, Goose Prairie neighbors of Justice William O. Douglas, for a Cougar Lakes Wilderness. **1966:** The area is one of three (Glacier Peak–Chelan and Alpine Lakes the other two) treated in the federal North Cascades Study Team Report. **1971:** A wilderness bill is introduced in Congress. **1976:** The North Cascades National Park having been created in 1968, and in this year the Alpine Lakes Wilderness, there is a general expectation that it is now the turn of the Cougar Lakes. **1983:** More bills have been introduced, yet still the wildland is left hanging, twisting slowly in the wind.

ALPINE LAKES WILDERNESS

When people in the young cities of Puget Sound and the Columbia River country felt the call of the frontier so recently lost, they typically banded together in large groups for summer outings of two weeks or more, veritable expeditions. As they gained experience, however, their craving for exploration grew too strong to be satisfied merely once a year. Accepting the opportunity for quick access presented by the railroad through Snoqualmie Pass, they became weekend mountaineers and then, with the improvement of automobiles and roads, Sunday wilderness walkers. For generations of climbers, hikers, fishermen, and Scouts who had never heard of Eldorado Peak— and who did not know there was a volcano in the Cascades between Rainier and Baker—their backyard wilderness was *the* wilderness.

The victory of 1976 made the Alpine Lakes the backyard of the nation. On the Pacific Crest National Scenic Trail between Snoqualmie Pass and Stevens Pass, a Washington hiker may in a single afternoon meet brethren from a dozen states, enraptured by the flower gardens of Kendall Peak or the big pines of the Waptus River, dazzled atop Surprise Mountain by Alaskan-seeming Mount Daniels, ecstatic from a first sighting of a mountain goat.

The wilderness traveler of Seattle or Yakima nowadays knows the Pickets and Flower Dome and Bailey Range, the Hanging Gardens and Whistler Basin and Avalanche Valley. But no matter how far he roams, he comes home to favorite backyard nooks, perhaps the wetland forests of Sunday Creek, highland forests of Commonwealth Basin, dry-land forests of Ingalls Creek, tundras of Snowgrass and Big Jim, towers of Chimney Rock and Bears Breast on the Cascade Crest, of the Cashmere Crags in the Stuart Range, and surely lakes, and lakes, and lakes.

Mountain goat

Penstemon

Prusik Peak and larches in the Alpine Lakes Wilderness

Reflection of Prusik Peak in Gnome Tarn

THE FOG
THAT REMAINS

It's a tough thing for a Puget Sound native to confess but sometimes there's almost more rain that I can truly love. Tramping the woods all day with half the Pacific Ocean in your shirt, that's great, that's what makes us who we are, happy as clams. But when night falls and the other half is in your sleeping bag a person can get melancholy.

Fog is another matter. Fog on the beach, the foghorns speaking the language of ghost ships. Fog in the forest, turning the trees to Japanese etchings. Fog in a meadow, a droplet sparkling on every lupine leaf. Fog around a campfire, giving you a shadow as huge as the Specter of the Brocken. Fog cools your brow and bathes your eyes and washes your whiskers and cleans the wax out of your ears. Sunshine makes smog from burned-up hydrocarbons, and the clear night sky glows with electricity from drowned rivers, but fog is what Shelley meant when he said, "The One remains, the many change and pass."

The other day I was at the courthouse listening to professional mouths tell the council why every American citizen has the inalienable right to ten shopping centers within five minutes of his carport. Afterward I drove home on the freeway with Grand Prix commuters perched on my rear bumper to show how angry they were that I was on the planet.

Everything was too much with me and I was ready to vote for the Bomb and something snapped and suddenly I was spreading my sleeping bag in the woods of Commonwealth Basin. The next morning I continued north along the Pacific Crest Trail, in the Alpine Lakes Wilderness. It's been said—notoriously by the Forest Service when it argued against putting the area in the Na-

tional Wilderness Preservation System—that this part of the Cascades is too popular to be truly wild in the old Leopold definition, or maybe even Zahniser's. Well, there's *solitude* wilderness and there's *sociable* wilderness. Personally, I need some of both. On this day especially it was very curative to meet folks from Omaha and Chicago and Hoboken, eyes shining because they'd seen their first bear grass and heard their first marmot whistle. Reminded me that the people in Schenectady and Dallas need the Alpine Lakes Wilderness as much as we do—or more. Also made me realize how much happier I am when I'm *liking* people. When he said, "In wildness is the preservation of the world," Thoreau said a mouthful.

I packed on past Ridge Lake and Bumblebee Pass, over the shoulder of Alaska and around the cirque of Joe Lake, to the saddle at the head of Gold Creek, between Huckleberry and Chikamin. I'd last been here in 1949, base-camping to climb all these peaks, and felt nostalgic. The afternoon sun was lazying so I lay in the short grass for auld lang syne—and woke up shivering.

Where did the fog sneak in from? The ocean, of course, where *we* snuck in from a few million years ago. We still don't belong in the sun. It hurts your eyes, dries your blood, wrinkles you like a Swiss ski instructor, makes you vote funny. It's not practical for us to dive back in the ocean and sing with the whales but fog is the next best thing. Fog is *home.*

I buttoned up my shirt and pulled my stocking cap down over my ears and lay in the grass feeling the fog wash over my nose and remembering the happy folks I'd met on the trail—new friends, friends forever, no matter how brief the encounter. I even began

Waterfall in the Alpine Lakes Wilderness

Sunset over Gold Creek in the Alpine Lakes Wilderness

*Mushroom and maple leaf
on "nurse log"*

forgiving the Grand Prix drivers on the freeway. You *know* why they're so burned up—they blame *you* for contributing to the overpopulation. You *know* why they're running so fast—because their old home was flattened to make a parking lot for a shopping center and it's too painful to search for their childhood and they're trying to find a place with no ghosts. You *know* why they're making such a racket—to drown out the sound of the future. They scurry like rats in a burning building from drive-in movies to tape decks to CB radio to rock to disco to theme parks to video games, from Swedish pancakes to quarter-pounders to Kentucky fried chicken to London fish and chips to Tijuana tacos to El Paso ribs. They're not *connected*. They're lost in space. They can't go home so they send out for pizza.

Well, we all feel lost a lot of the time. How is a person to navigate when our mental maps, the ones we learned growing up, are years out of date, and the new maps cranked out as regularly as newspapers by the land developers and the highway departments are weird as Mars and twice as anti-human?

That's when places like Gold Creek saddle help. Despite the trail, which by now had been here quite a few years, it looked about the same as 1949. Thousands of people, instead of three or four, were coming through every summer. But they were *caring* folks, and they were *taking* care—the hikers from Hoboken who couldn't live there unless this was here, the wilderness rangers whose heroes are Aldo Leopold and Bob Marshall.

When I was little we used to camp at a spot some distance out of Enumclaw on a dirt road, under a Douglas fir so big it took me and my folks and all the available aunts and uncles and cousins to link hands around it. One year we found the tree had fallen, and us kids had great sport clambering the roots up to the trunk and walking that high avenue, strutting like kings and queens. Another year we found the CCC at work turning our camp into The Dalles Campground. Several years ago I stopped by on a

sentimental journey and could tell a few million kids had been playing on the log.

It had been sawn through for a nature trail, so people could count the rings. I counted, and calculated the tree was a seedling when my great-great-great-etcetera grandparents were fighting for—and against—King Alfred. That log—it's still there—connects me to King Alfred, and to my childhood, and to my parents and aunts and uncles and cousins, and to the folks who built the Pyramids and Stonehenge, and to the bears and the dinosaurs and the whales. The log is nursing a row of hemlocks, now. Maybe after the fir has rotted to duff, sunk into the forest floor, my great-great-great-etcetera grandchildren will come to admire the hemlock colonnade—and maybe feel connected to me.

•　　•　　•

The day was too far gone to cross Alta Pass to the next recommended cámpsite, and I hoped the wilderness rangers would forgive me for declaring an emergency and staying at a spot too fragile for camping. I didn't really camp, just rested overnight. Ate cheese and crackers and drank orange juice. Spread mattress and bag on a rock and crawled in and wrapped up in a plastic tablecloth and went to sleep listening to fog. You have to listen close.

I awoke in mists hissing through soggy hemlocks. Looked up to beads of water strung along the branches, getting fatter, falling to splash on my tablecloth.

I crawled out and ate a piece of chocolate while packing, then hiked from the saddle up to the long green wall of Chikamin. The flowers were in climax and wouldn't let me walk fast. I had to spend time at the cushions of moss dotted with the bright yellow blossoms of alpine monkey flower and the tiny violet crosses of alpine willow herb and little glittering globules of accumulated fog.

At Alta Pass I crossed the ridge to East Side sun. But before drying out and warming up I paused to fill my lungs with the cold, gray ocean. Where I came from.

Forest floor in Little Beaver Valley

Vine maple in the Big Beaver Valley

Winter cascade in the Mount Baker Area

Huckleberry leaf and larch needles

Winter-clad Mount Rainier and Tipsoo Lake

North Fork Skykomish River in the Glacier Peak Additions

Blacktail deer

Yarrow leaf and dew

PART III

The Next Decade/
The Next Century

THE UNFINISHED WORK

by Richard Rutz

SAVING OUR HERITAGE:
A PROPOSAL FOR WASHINGTON WILDERNESS

A number of local, state, and national citizens' groups have worked to develop a Washington wilderness proposal that incorporates the finest, most important wild and roadless areas still remaining in our state. These groups include:

Alpine Lakes Protection Society
Black Canyon Society
Boeing Employees Alpine Society, Seattle
Boulder River Protection Association
Citizens for Responsible Water Projects, Yakima
Climbing Club, University of Washington, Seattle
Colville Valley Environmental Council
Environmental Law Caucus, Spokane
Federation of Western Outdoor Clubs
Friends of the Clearwater, Tacoma
Friends of Cypress Island, Anacortes
Friends of the Earth
Friends of Glacier Peak, Everett
Friends of the Juniper Forest, Walla Walla
Glacier Peak Wilderness Watch, Wenatchee
Higgins Mountain Protection Society
Hood Canal Environmental Council, Seabeck
Indian Heaven Alliance
Intermountain Alpine Club, Richland
Issaquah Alps Trails Club, Issaquah
Kettle Range Conservation Group, Republic
Kettle River Preservation Society, Orient
Mount Baker Wilderness Association, Bellingham
Mount St. Helens Protective Association
The Mountaineers, Seattle, Everett, Tacoma,
  Olympia, Bellingham
National Audubon Society
North Cascades Conservation Council
Okanogan Wilderness League, Carlton
Olympic Park Associates
Salmo-Priest Defense Fund
Seattle Audubon Society
Sierra Club
The Wilderness Society
Washington Environmental Council
Washington Wilderness Coalition
Washington Wildlife Study Council, Seattle
Whitman Environmental Action Coalition,
  Walla Walla
Willapa Hills Audubon Society

The fight to save Washington's wild heritage, begun so long ago, still continues. Even as we go to press, the congressional delegation is considering which of the unprotected roadless lands should be included in the wilderness system. Your views are important: contact your elected officials (see *WHAT YOU CAN DO*) and let them know that you support a wilderness bill that includes any or all of the following areas and recommended sizes.

OLYMPIC (CANAL FRONT, WONDER MOUNTAIN, COLONEL BOB/SOUTH QUINAULT RIDGE, PINE MOUNTAIN, STORMKING MOUNTAIN, BALDY RIDGE, McDONALD MOUNTAIN)
Location: Several units on the north, east, and south sides of Olympic National Park in northwestern Washington, in the Olympic National Forest (see figure 1).
Size: 135,000 acres
The Canal Front areas in the eastern portion of the Olympic proposal include several popular climbing peaks (The Brothers, Mount Washington and Mount Ellinor), lakes (Mildred Lakes and Lena Lake), and a number of well-used trails. Central to the proposal are several rivers that are of great importance to maintaining wild runs of salmon and trout, and which also provide important wildlife habitat and recreational opportunities along their banks: the Gray Wolf, Dungeness, Quilcene, Dosewallips, Duckabush, and Hamma Hamma rivers. Much of the area is unforested, and most of the forested lands have thin, erodable soils (which can and are destroying the nearby fisheries where logging is occurring) and major reforestation problems. Proposed hydroelectric projects threaten the fish runs on several of these rivers. Wonder Mountain-Skokomish River contains a popular recreational area with high fish and wildlife habitat values and has little worthwhile timber. Colonel Bob/South Quinault Ridge supplies water to the recreationally significant Quinault River and Lake Quinault and to their fisheries; only part of the southern end of this area contains significant timber. Pine Mountain is a small area (320-acre) that the Forest Service plans to clear-cut; this could cause soil erosion that would foul the Bogachiel River in the

Overleaf - *Mount Baker from Winchester Mountain*

OLYMPIC

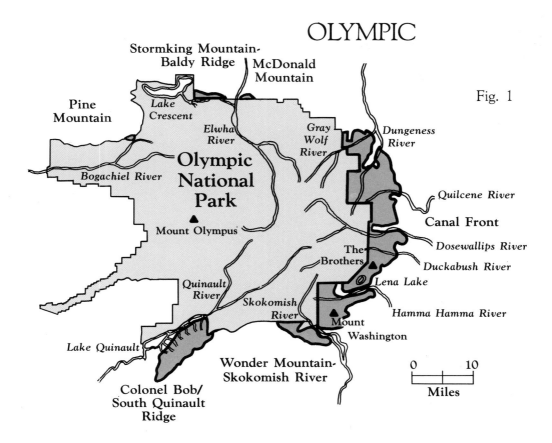

Fig. 1

national park. Stormking Mountain, Baldy Ridge, and McDonald Mountain to the north contribute to the Lake Crescent, Barnes River, and Elwha River drainages in the park; their designation as wilderness is needed in order to protect the park's river systems.

PATOS ISLAND
Location: Several small islets and rocks in Puget Sound, in northwestern Washington
Size: 200 acres
The Coast Guard's Little Patos Island is fifteen acres of valuable marine habitat. Together with portions of Patos Island and various other small islets, the proposal would complement the existing 353-acre San Juan Islands Wilderness.

MOUNT BAKER (TWIN SISTERS, NOISY-DIOBSUD, AND TOMYHOI-SILESIA AREAS)
Location: Northwestern Cascades, in the Mount Baker–Snoqualmie National Forest (see figure 2).
Size: 245,000 acres
Komo Kulshan, the ancient mountain god of the Northwest Washington Indians, looks down upon a wilderness of fifty lakes, forty major peaks, and dozens of valleys in his domain. A wide variety of recreational opportunities are available to the young

and old, including picnicking, horse riding, hiking, and climbing. The Twin Sisters support an unusual plant community, while the undisturbed forests and valleys in several areas still support wildlife that elsewhere has been eliminated by human activities. The undisturbed forests also are important to Indian religious observances. Glacier-fed streams supply water to the various branches of the Nooksack River; this river and others (such as Noisy, Swift, and Diobsud creeks) provide habitat for many of the area's fish runs. Fish and wildlife habitat as well as many recreational and cultural values will be harmed by logging if these wildlands remain unprotected: even the Mount Baker Recreational Area is scheduled for logging. Saving these trees need have no significant effect on neighboring areas: the Forest Service's annual unsold volume for the bordering lands exceeds the potential harvest from the proposed wilderness. Furthermore, cutting trees in the proposed wilderness would cost more money than it would make. Geothermal development also poses potential conflict, but it could probably be relocated outside of the proposal. Planned expansion of the downhill ski facility will not be affected. Off-road vehicle trails and a mineral area have been excluded from the proposed wilderness.

125

MOUNT BAKER

Fig. 2

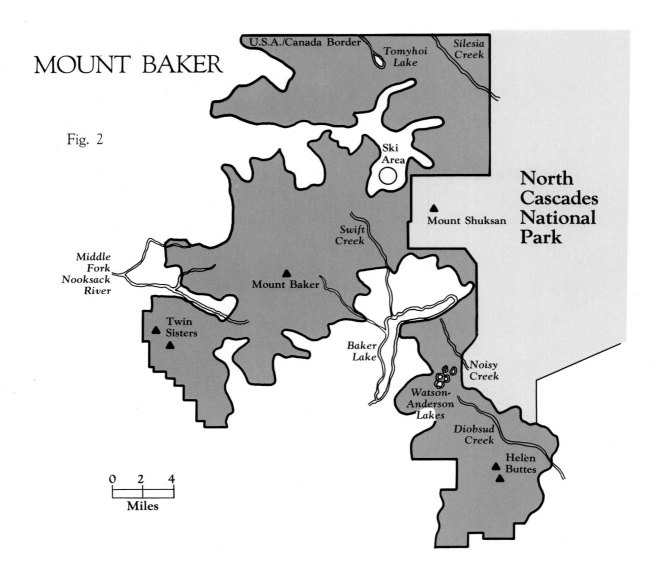

U.S.A./Canada Border

Tomyhoi
Lake

Silesia
Creek

Ski
Area

**North
Cascades
National
Park**

▲
Mount Shuksan

Swift
Creek

Middle
Fork
Nooksack
River

▲
Mount Baker

Twin
Sisters
▲
▲

Baker
Lake

Noisy
Creek

Watson-
Anderson
Lakes

Diobsud
Creek

Helen
Buttes
▲
▲

0   2   4
Miles

ALMA COPPER-HIDDEN LAKE

Location: Northwestern Washington, on the west side of the North Cascades National Park, in the Mount Baker–Snoqualmie National Forest

Size: 13,000 acres

Tributaries of the Skagit and Cascade rivers (federally designated scenic and recreational rivers) flow from these lands, including Copper Creek with its important habitat for bald eagles and anadromous fish. Each area contains scenic trails that overlook or provide access to the national park. Hydroelectric development on the streams is the major threat, with some logging contemplated on the lower slopes.

GLACIER PEAK ADDITIONS

Location: North Cascades, in the Mount Baker–Snoqualmie National Forest (see figure 3).

Size: 590,000 acres

In an attempt to provide adequate protection for

the important lands that surround but are not included in the existing wilderness, conservation and other groups support additions along most of the periphery of the wilderness. A wide variety of recreational trails leading into the wilderness is found in these additions; on the east side, the trails are threatened by reconstruction into motorcycle paths. In areas where there are trees, logging (much of it unprofitable) is scheduled, with concurrent loss of trail mileage, scenery, and wildlife and fish habitat. Many fish streams and habitats would be harmed by the sediment resulting from this logging. In particular, the superlative Lake Janus-Lake Valhalla-Rapid River area north of Stevens Pass, a recreational favorite, would be severely harmed by logging. Mineralized lands in the additions have not proved economical to develop and should not be a major conflict. Hydroelectric proposals, however, are proliferating here, threatening many of the resources and values.

GLACIER PEAK ADDITIONS

Fig. 3

Cascade River

Big Creek

Buck Creek

Glacier Peak Wilderness

Suiattle River

0   5
Miles

▲ *Mount Pugh*

▲ *Glacier Peak*

Lake Chelan

North Fork Entiat River

▲
Sloan Peak

Rock Creek

Big Four Mountain

▲ *Monte Cristo Peak*

Entiat River

Blanca Lake

Skykomish River

Ragged Ridge

Heather Lake

Grizzly Peak ▲

▲ *Dirtyface Peak*

Mad River

Rapid River

Lake Janus

Lake Wenatchee

Lake Valhalla

HIGGINS MOUNTAIN

Location: West of the main Cascades in northwestern Washington, in the Mount Baker–Snoqualmie National Forest

Size: 13,000 acres

Rising prominently above Highway 530 leading east to Darrington, the south face of Higgins Mountain sweeps up in a broad arc from the alder and Douglas-fir forest of the Stillaguamish River valley to the rocky summit ridge. Screened from the highway, on the north side of the mountain, is a popular area of forested slopes, alpine meadows, and ponds. The timber values are low: logging on nearby lands has resulted in a number of slides that have harmed valuable fisheries, and reforestation of these areas has been difficult.

BOULDER RIVER-MOUNT DICKERMAN

Location: North-central Washington, west of the main Cascades, in the Mount Baker–Snoqualmie National Forest

Size: 80,000 acres

Within an hour of Everett is the Boulder River area, a favorite of hikers, climbers, school classes, families, and hunters. Deep valleys hide rare plants, and lush vegetation supports wildlife in abundance. Clear waters supply the fish-spawning grounds of the Sauk and Stillaguamish rivers.

The supreme attribute of the proposed wilderness is the Boulder River valley, one of the last unlogged valleys in the Cascades. A nearly level trail up the valley is very popular. The forest of the valley is eyed by some, but its wood is inferior, roading costs would be prohibitively high, and extremely unstable soils and clay underlie much of it. Logging in most of the valley would be terribly damaging, and would consist of money-losing sales.

EAGLE ROCK

Location: Central Cascades, north of Highway 2 and the Index area, in the Mount Baker–Snoqualmie National Forest

Size: 34,000 acres

This steep mountain expanse is dominated by vertical cliffs rising to the impressive summits of Mount Baring, Spire Mountain, and others. Deeply incised

127

valleys lead to the many lakes (including Barclay) that are popular with fishermen and hikers. Although most of the meager timber resource is unsuitable for logging (soil instability and regeneration problems are great), logging and roads threaten further to reduce trail mileage and to harm the recreational resource.

NASON RIDGE
Location: A spur from the eastern slope of the central Cascades, in the Wenatchee National Forest
Size: 21,000 acres
Rugged and rocky Nason Ridge forms a colorful backdrop to Lake Wenatchee. Steep, unstable slopes frequently avalanche in winter, but flame with color in the autumn. The twenty-six-mile Nason Ridge Trail is a favorite of hikers who seek the views from its open highlands, and cross-country skiers use many parts of it for winter touring. Timbered streams and lakes in the lower elevations provide habitat for birds and other animals. The timber is generally sparse and of minimal value.

DEVIL'S GULCH
Location: Eastern end of the Wenatchee Mountains on the east side of the central Washington Cascades, in the Wenatchee National Forest
Size: 14,000 acres
Mixed conifer and lodgepole pine forest, which will not support long-term timber management, is scattered on the mountain slopes and benches of Devil's Gulch, with sagebrush in the canyon bottoms. Water for irrigation and orchards and habitat for elk, raptors, grouse, and other wildlife are provided here. Hunting, horseback riding, hiking, and skiing are favored recreational activities that conflict with off-road vehicle use of portions of the area.

LAKE CHELAN-SAWTOOTH DIVIDE
Location: North and east of Lake Chelan on the eastern side of the Cascades, in the Okanogan and Wenatchee national forests
Size: 310,000 acres
First proposed for protection near the turn of the century by the residents of Chelan, the Lake Chelan-Sawtooth Divide provides excellent hiking, horse riding, fishing, hunting, and cross-country skiing opportunities in a country where sharp, barren peaks and ridges are juxtaposed with the green of the valleys and the blue of the lake. Off-road vehicles menace the fragile uplands of the Sawtooth Divide, while logging is planned for the approach valleys. Helicopter skiing, planned for a few areas, threatens already pressured wildlife with further harassment. The portion of the proposal in Granite

Creek has no significant use conflicts: its trees must stay in order to preserve the scenery along the North Cascades Highway.

BLACK CANYON
Location: Southeastern end of Sawtooth Ridge, east of Lake Chelan in the Okanogan National Forest
Size: 13,600 acres
The main stream of Black Canyon, Black Canyon Creek, flows through a forested valley immediately adjacent to the sagebrush flats of the Columbia Basin. Hunting and hiking are popular in this area that provides key winter range for mule deer and habitat for bears, golden eagles, blue grouse, and other animals. Black Canyon is also among the best entrances to the Sawtooth Ridge for cross-country skiers. Motorcycles and logging are the chief threats.

PASAYTEN WILDERNESS ADDITIONS (INCLUDING CHEWACK/TWENTY MILE-THIRTY MILE, GOLDEN HORN, FAREWELL CREEK, LOST RIVER, AND LONG DRAW)
Location: North-central Washington, along the southern and eastern periphery of the Pasayten Wilderness in the Okanogan National Forest
Size: 210,000 acres
These areas along the wilderness periphery provide approach routes and also have significant recreational values in their own right. Twenty Mile-Thirty Mile also contains a high plateau and untouched watershed from which nearby residents obtain a quality water supply. There is important habitat for deer, elk, cougars, marten, bears, lynx, and other animals. Timber resources are submarginal and uneconomical to log, and consist to a large extent of the poorly marketable lodgepole pine.

TIFFANY
Location: North-central Washington, in the Okanogan National Forest
Size: 25,000 acres
The Tiffany Mountain area is principally high-elevation land, with grassy meadows and timberline ecosystems. Tiffany Lake has good fishing for cutthroat trout, and the land provides good habitat for mule deer and moose. The fine ridge walks and 360-degree vista from Tiffany Mountain lure hikers. Logging the generally marginal and submarginal timber would waste money and harm these resources.

BEAVER MEADOWS
Location: North-central Washington, in the Okanogan National Forest
Size: 38,000 acres
A sweep of broken terrain, the ridges of Beaver

Meadows provide recreational opportunities, wildlife habitat, and important watershed for a dry region of the state. Removal of the rather sparse tree cover would lessen the water retention of the soil and would exacerbate flooding (which is already a problem in this part of the state after the infrequent rains).

CHOPAKA MOUNTAIN
Location: North-central Washington, on Bureau of Land Management lands
Size: 5,000 acres
The Chopaka Mountain expanse has very rugged terrain (most prominently a 6,700-foot scarp). Grazing use is the major conflict, but this occurs in only a portion of the area and could be accommodated. Timber resources are minuscule, and the few mineral deposits are uneconomical to develop. Unusual plant communities lie in some of its gullies.

OKANOGAN HIGHLANDS
Location: Northern Washington, midway between the Cascades and Idaho, shared by the Okanogan and Colville national forests
Size: Four units—Jackson Creek, Clackamas Mountain-Maple Mountain, Mount Bonaparte, and Dugout—totaling 44,000 acres
The generally rough and broken terrain of the Okanogan Highlands gives refuge to many wildlife species, and helps to secure the opportunity for solitude. The many streams provide important habitat for fish and supply high-quality water for agricultural lands. The moderate timber resources provide a spurious conflict with recreational use of the areas, for the trees generally stand on unstable soils that are unsuitable for logging.

KETTLE RANGE
Location: A mountain range running north to south from the Canadian border to the Columbia Plateau, in the Colville National Forest in northeastern Washington
Size: Four units—Bald-Snow, Thirteen Mile, Profanity, and Twin Sisters—totaling 94,000 acres
Grassy, open forest and numerous meadows dot the rolling peaks and windswept crest of the Kettle Range. Recreational use here is great, ranging from family outings to extended backpacking trips. Cross-country skiing is a favorite winter sport. There is superb winter range for deer and habitat for fish, wildlife, and threatened plant species. The Kettle Range also provides important watershed for the extremely dry neighboring region.

The combination of high elevation and dry climate makes most of the Kettle Range's timber unprofitable to manage on a sustained-yield basis. Log-

ging would sacrifice the many benefits here to what would be a one-time timber venture. It is, moreover, unnecessary to log, for the Colville National Forest undersells its harvest potential. By programming the unsold volume, the output of the three neighboring counties could be increased above present levels, even after the designation of the Kettle Range, Salmo-Priest, and Abercrombie-Hooknose areas as wilderness.

ABERCROMBIE-HOOKNOSE
Location: Northeastern Washington, in the Colville National Forest
Size: 37,000 acres
Burned-over forest and grassy slopes on rounded, mature mountains characterize most of the Abercrombie-Hooknose. Hiking, hunting, and camping are the primary recreational uses, and the area also supports bears, deer, elk, and many other animals. Timber is the main, but wholly unnecessary, conflict (see *Kettle Range*). Colville National Forest is exceptional in the Pacific Northwest because it has a very low recreational-to-timber land ratio (only 6 percent of the land is given to recreational uses, while 94 percent is devoted to timber). Designation of the Abercrombie-Hooknose, Kettle Range, and Salmo-Priest as wilderness would bring the recreational land base to a more balanced 18 percent.

SALMO-PRIEST
Location: Northeastern corner of Washington and northwestern tip of Idaho, in the Colville and Idaho Panhandle national forests
Size: 75,420 acres
The Salmo-Priest is one of the finest wildlife areas in Washington state. A great diversity of game and nongame wildlife species make their home here, including several threatened species and the endangered mountain caribou. Important fish streams flow into the Salmo and Priest rivers from the high alpine country. The abundant moisture supports a climax cedar forest in the lower lands—a favorite of hikers, and critical habitat for wildlife species.

The forest is also the source of the major threat, logging. Many crucial fish and wildlife and recreational areas were left out of the Forest Service's wilderness recommendations, principally so that timber sales could be programmed in the excluded sections. Analysis of the timber and recreation supply situation (see *Kettle Range* and *Abercrombie-Hooknose*) shows that wilderness designation of the Salmo-Priest need not adversely affect the timber supply of the neighboring counties, and would meet an acute need for more recreational lands in the Colville National Forest.

JUNIPER FOREST

Location: Southeastern Washington, near Richland, on Bureau of Land Management land

Size: 7,000 acres

Also known as the Juniper Dunes, the area is a scene of shifting sand dunes, sage-steppe plant communities, and six groves and scattered groups of unmerchantable juniper trees. These trees provide habitat for up to half of the nesting pairs of ferruginous hawks in Washington, and for many other animals. Hikers and hunters frequent the Juniper Forest, and many schools visit on field trips and for environmental studies. Wild flowers attract many people as well. The threat comes from off-road vehicles, which have been extending their range into the Juniper Forest.

GOAT ROCKS ADDITIONS

Location: South-central Cascades in the Wenatchee and Gifford Pinchot national forests

Size: 35,000 acres

The Goat Rocks Wilderness additions would provide more natural boundaries to the wilderness and would protect most of the approach trails. Logging would shorten most of these trails and would harm camping sites; geothermal leasing is another possible conflict. Threatened expansion of the downhill ski permit area in White Pass poses a major threat to the Pacific Crest Trail and some of the additions, as well as to the wilderness itself.

DARK DIVIDE-BLUE LAKE

Location: Southwestern Washington between Mount Adams and Mount St. Helens, in the Gifford Pinchot National Forest

Size: Two units, 73,000-acre Dark Divide and 10,000-acre Blue Lake

An island beauty in a sea of clearcuts, the Dark Divide includes such peaks as Shark Rock and Spencer Butte, and the magnificent low-elevation forest of Quartz Creek Valley. The Blue Lake unit is centered on a secluded basin that contains the lake and is enclosed by high, windswept ridges. The high ridges are not jeopardized, but the forested portions are slated for logging. The heavily roaded Gifford Pinchot Forest has a great need for the preservation of roadless areas that include low-elevation forest; this proposal can in part meet the need.

TRAPPER CREEK

Location: Southwestern Washington, in the Gifford Pinchot National Forest

Size: 10,000 acres

The Trapper Creek proposal incorporates the last major unlogged valley in the southern portion of the Pinchot Forest. The area is bounded by the rocky summits of Sisters Rocks and other peaks, and has several important trails. Much of the land is mantled with old-growth Pacific silver fir and Douglas fir (mostly on steeply sloping land), but much is still recovering from a large burn in 1910. Steep slopes and reforestation problems suggest that long-term timber management is not economical for most of the forest.

BIG LAVA BED

Location: Southwestern Washington, in the Gifford Pinchot National Forest

Size: 20,000 acres

This expanse hosts an outstanding geological feature, a sparsely vegetated lava bed covering more than fifteen square miles. The Pacific Crest Trail runs along its western side and down into the Big Huckleberry Mountain area. The soil is thin and fragile throughout this country, and timber resources are meager. The spectacular wild-flower gardens at Grassy Knoll are among the finest in the Northwest.

MOUNT ADAMS ADDITIONS

Location: South Cascades, in the Gifford Pinchot National Forest

Size: 28,000 acres

When the Mount Adams Wild Area (later designated as wilderness) was established, the snowfields and meadows were protected, but few of the trees were included. The additions would protect the views, several trail approaches, and several miles of the Pacific Crest Trail and the Round-the-Mountain Trail. The additions would also include some badly needed wooded areas; proposed logging would eliminate these last forested stands.

INDIAN HEAVEN

Location: Southwestern Washington, in the Gifford Pinchot National Forest

Size: 28,000 acres

Indian Heaven is a highland of gentle contours cloaked in subalpine forest and meadow, throughout which are scattered more than two hundred ponds and lakes. An Indian meeting and gathering place for centuries, it is now a favorite of hikers (the area includes fourteen miles of the Pacific Crest Trail), horse riders, campers, and berry-pickers. Several Forest Service plans have extolled the virtues of Indian Heaven and have recommended protection, but the area has nevertheless shrunk to less than half of the size it had in 1962. Oil and gas leasing threatens some portions, and current plans call for reducing its size by more than seven thou-

OUGAR LAKES-NORSE PEAK
GREENWATER RIVER

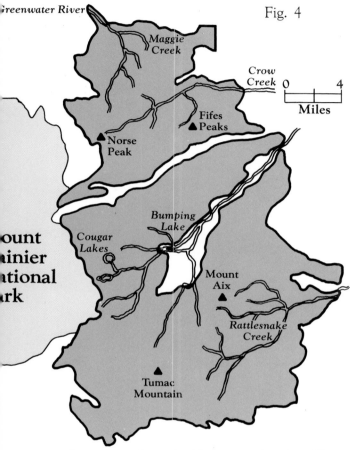

Greenwater River

Maggie Creek

Crow Creek

Fig. 4

0   4

Miles

Fifes Peaks

Norse Peak

Bumping Lake

Cougar Lakes

Mount Rainier National Park

Mount Aix

Rattlesnake Creek

Tumac Mountain

sand acres in order to log the marginal timber. The sales would not meet costs and would destroy the value of much of this unique land.

CLEARWATER

Location: West of the Cascades and north of Mount Rainier National Park, in the Mount Baker-Snoqualmie National Forest

Size: 24,000 acres

The Clearwater roadless area holds the headwaters of several rivers; magnificent patriarchal trees line the river in stands that surpass those of the national park. These same trees provide habitat for big game and many other wildlife species. Recreationists of all sorts are drawn to the trees, the high meadows, and the famous views of Mount Rainier. A favorite of Tacoma city residents, the Clearwater helps to relieve the recreational pressure on the national park. The timber here forms a negligible portion of the neighboring county's base, and most of it is of marginal quality or prohibitively expensive to log and manage.

TATOOSH-GLACIER VIEW

Location: South (Tatoosh) and west (Glacier View) of Mount Rainier National Park, on the west side of the central Cascades, in the Gifford Pinchot National Forest

Size: Two units totaling 26,000 acres

The plateau country and rocky ridges of Glacier View provide some of the finest vistas of The Mountain. Timber is a potential use conflict in a portion of the area, but the volume involved is small. An off-road vehicle area is near, providing another potential conflict. Tatoosh incorporates land previously proposed by the Forest Service for addition to the park. It includes part of the Tatoosh Range, and the Muddy Fork of the Cowlitz River, a Wild and Scenic River candidate. The Forest Service proposes to snip away at the edges, removing the few easily reached forested acres.

COUGAR LAKES-NORSE PEAK-
GREENWATER RIVER

Location: Central portion of the Cascade Range east of Mount Rainier National Park, in the Wenatchee and Mount Baker–Snoqualmie national forests (see figure 4).

Size: Two units, totaling 257,000 acres

The Cougar Lakes are a recreational paradise, with more than two hundred miles of scenic trails. Included are the Pacific Crest Trail, along the entire western length of the area, and the beautiful Greenwater River Trail, one of the most popular trails in the state for all ages. Wildlife and fish are abundant, thanks to large expanses of undisturbed habitat. The area also provides a significant portion of the water for the Yakima drainage for agriculture (the most important economic activity in Yakima County), fisheries, and urban use.

Timber supply is the principal conflict. However, with the exception of a few heavily forested valleys, long-term timber values are low due to poor soils and an unfavorable climate. Analysis of the timber supply situation reveals that less than 2 percent of the local counties' harvests would be affected; moreover, neither the Forest Service nor the Bureau of Indian Affairs can sell enough timber to meet their allowable cuts. Nonetheless, timber sales are planned here, including major portions of the Norse Peak and Greenwater areas. The superb wilderness values should not be sacrificed to such a dubious end. As Justice William O. Douglas stated, logging the Cougar Lakes would be an act of "official vandalism."

Other threats and conflicts are present, too. Most motorcycle routes have been carefully excluded from the wilderness proposal, but some motorcycles disturb the lower Greenwater, and a few snowmobiles have pushed up onto the Tumac Plateau. The Bureau of Reclamation has proposed enlarging Bumping Lake reservoir (at a benefit to cost ratio of 0.6:1) and has also proposed another dam in Rattlesnake Creek. Wilderness designation is the only classification that can protect the Cougar Lakes and their many values and uses from these threats.

ISSAQUAH ALPS NATIONAL URBAN RECREATION AREA
Location: Near Issaquah, on the west side of the central Cascades
Size: Not yet specified
The Issaquah Alps are located east of Seattle, ringing the small community of Issaquah. Consisting of peaks ranging from 1,600 to 3,000 feet in elevation,
the Issaquah Alps are a refuge within the expanding urban center of Western Washington. *Not* a wilderness proposal, the proposed recreation area is mostly forested in second-growth, with some large relict patches of virgin forest. Several high-quality creeks support the most important urban fisheries in the nation. The Issaquah Alps Trails Club, The Mountaineers, and other allied groups support a National Urban Recreation Area, under the jurisdiction of the National Park Service. The Park Service would oversee the lands and coordinate planning and management among the various private and public ownerships and local governments. It would arrange for easements, land purchases, and zoning regulations to protect the watershed, wildlife and fisheries, and other qualities of this urban wildland.

WILDERNESS MYTHS AND MISCONCEPTIONS

There are a number of misunderstandings and misconceptions about wilderness that are often exploited by wilderness opponents.

MYTH 1: Wilderness is a single use that conflicts with multiple-use legislation.
Wilderness is recognized—rightly—in legislation, along with outdoor recreation, range, wildlife and fish, timber, and watersheds as a viable form of multiple use. Wilderness areas preserve wildlife and fish habitats and populations and act as genetic reservoirs for all of the living organisms that are found there. Wilderness protects watersheds, provides forage for livestock, and offers opportunities for recreation that are free from motors and in which the number of encounters with other people is low. Logging is the only one of the listed uses that is not permitted in wilderness (beginning in 1984, new mineral claims may not be filed, but old claims will continue to be recognized), for logging and its associated roading have too often shown themselves destructive of ecosystems.

MYTH 2: Wilderness is elitist: only a tiny minority of people use wilderness areas.
Wilderness, park, and roadless area use is heavy and is increasing rapidly. The Forest Service has estimated that if all of its (miserly) recommendations for wilderness are enacted for Washington and Oregon, capacity for recreation on these lands will still be reached by 1985! The Mountaineers schedules most of its trips in wilderness and roadless areas, as do many others who fish, hunt, hike, camp, collect rocks, or observe nature. Many other people
benefit from and "use" wilderness indirectly, feeling better knowing that wilderness still exists. This is as true of the person who decides to live in Washington because of "the quality of life and the fine environment" as it is of the person who is concerned with providing habitat protection for wildlife and fish populations.

Wilderness recreation is inexpensive when compared with sports such as alpine skiing, snowmobiling, motorcycling, or motorboating. It also takes no more time to enjoy it than to participate in many other leisure activities. Designated wilderness areas or the areas in this wilderness proposal can be reached from any metropolis in the state within a couple of hours.

Wilderness need not be restricted to the hardy and fit. The Boulder River and Greenwater trails (both in this wilderness proposal), for example, are lowland trails that old and young, fit and unfit, individuals and families can enjoy. The threat comes from relegating and limiting wilderness to high elevation "rock and ice" areas, where it *would* be largely limited to the fit. The wilderness proposal described in this book will provide a wide range of opportunities.

MYTH 3: Wilderness designation prevents forest fire and pest control and impedes emergency access.
The Wilderness Act specifically allows control of fire, insects, and disease that would harm timber outside of the wilderness: for example, within the last few years a fire in the Pasayten Wilderness was fought with mechanized equipment. Fires and infes-

tations that pose no threat to outside resources are allowed, for they are a vital part of natural ecosystems. Motorized equipment also is allowed for emergencies involving human health and safety, and is so used.

MYTH 4: Wild areas must be virgin and pristine in order to qualify for wilderness.
Since 1964 Congress has repeatedly rejected overly strict purity standards, recognizing that there is no "pure" wilderness remaining today. The Wilderness Act defines wilderness as "land retaining its primeval character and influence...and which *generally* appears to have been affected *primarily* by the forces of nature, with the imprint of man's work substantially unnoticeable" (emphasis added). The essential point is that certain past actions may be tolerated or corrected, but similar disturbing actions may not be initiated in a wilderness.

Wilderness also need not be completely insulated from the "sights and sounds" of man's activities. The "sights and sounds" criterion is a tactic that is used to minimize the amount of land that can be considered for wilderness: it is especially useful when managers seek to exclude lowland forests and approach routes from wilderness consideration. Glimpses of logging roads in the distance or the sounds of activities occurring outside of an area are *not* valid reasons for excluding it from wilderness consideration. Such "sights and sounds" have only a small effect on a visitor's appreciation for wildland; in fact, they often foster a greater appreciation for land that is still unaltered.

MYTH 5: Wilderness removes valuable timberland from production and costs jobs.
Wilderness designation precludes the use of an area for timber harvest, and it is therefore important to analyze how this wilderness proposal will affect current timber supplies. It is also important to consider the many benefits—wildlife and fish habitat protection, watershed and water-quality protection, opportunities for primitive recreation, retention of genetic diversity, and many others—that wilderness provides. These valuable benefits can well overcome the small reductions in timber output that result from this wilderness proposal. The wilderness proposal in this book can be in part the mechanism for a return to the true multiple use of our national forests.

Impact on Timber Land Base and Harvest Volume
Commercial forest land (CFL) produces twenty or more cubic feet of wood fiber per acre per year. Of the statewide total of 17,567,000 acres of CFL available for harvest in 1983, only 3.9 percent is in

our wilderness proposal (see table 1). Wilderness designation would have a similar small effect on the statewide harvest volume. The average annual harvest for Washington (1970–1980) is 6,718 million board feet (a board foot is a volume of wood 12 inches long, 12 inches wide and 1 inch thick). The wilderness proposal, if completely enacted, would reduce the potential annual harvest from available lands by 3.0 percent (see table 2).

It is clear that the many benefits of wilderness can be secured for a relatively small cost to the statewide timber supply. This cost could, furthermore, be more than compensated for by properly reforesting many acres of previously harvested forest land: more than a billion acres of CFL in Washington are not currently reforested or are poorly reforested (Washington Department of Natural Resources *Forest Productivity Study*, 1982; U.S. Forest Service *General Technical Report PNW-60*, 1975).

Impact on Employment
The reduction in timber volume due to the designation of wilderness would have some effect on employment in forest products industries. However, many more jobs are lost each year as a result of the export of logs for processing overseas. The annual average volume (1970–1980) of exported logs is 1,967 million board feet, more than *nine times* the impact the entire wilderness proposal would have (see table 3). Table 4 shows that domestic processing of logs into lumber, plywood, and veneer provides two to four times the number of jobs that logging alone provides.

Employment in forest products industries is cyclical, showing significant short- and long-term fluctuations. These fluctuations in employment levels are much greater than the impact that would result from wilderness designation (see table 3). Table 5 shows that this fluctuation is directly related to the condition of the national economy (as indicated by new housing starts).

Timber Benefits from Wilderness Designation
Among the many benefits that wilderness provides are several for the timber resource. A more reliable, evenly distributed supply of water is one. Wilderness protection of forests in the headwaters helps to prevent soil erosion and helps to retain water quality and soil productivity both in the headwaters and downstream. Water is released in a more even flow over a longer period than when the land is bare and water runs off rapidly.

Preservation of genetic diversity is another important benefit. It cannot be emphasized too strongly that the Pacific Northwest is a major producer of

133

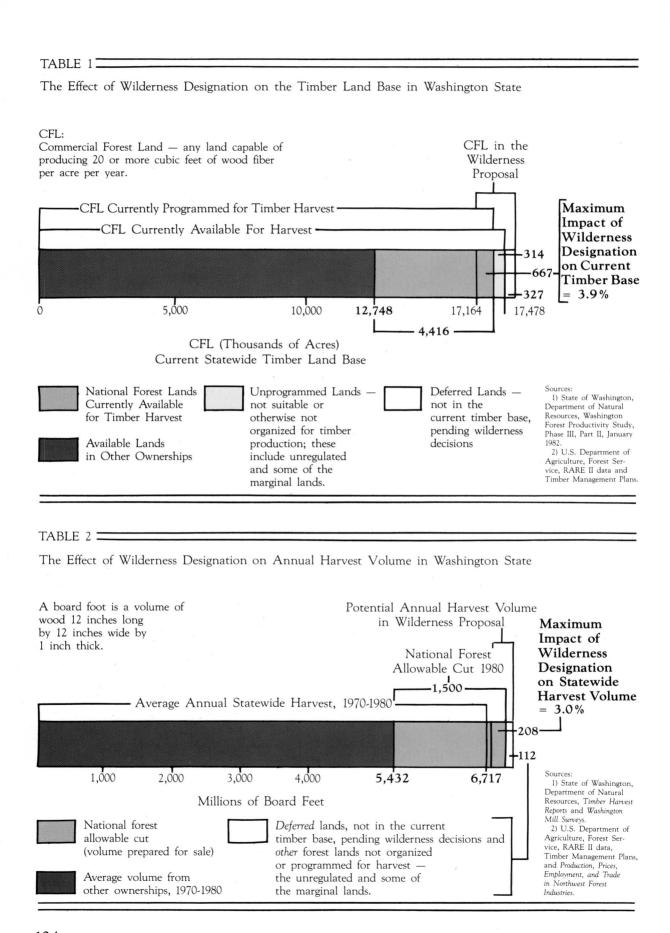

TABLE 1

The Effect of Wilderness Designation on the Timber Land Base in Washington State

CFL:
Commercial Forest Land — any land capable of
producing 20 or more cubic feet of wood fiber
per acre per year.

CFL in the
Wilderness
Proposal

CFL Currently Programmed for Timber Harvest

CFL Currently Available For Harvest

Maximum
Impact of
Wilderness
Designation
on Current
Timber Base
= 3.9%

314

667

327

0   5,000   10,000   12,748   17,164   17,478

CFL (Thousands of Acres)
Current Statewide Timber Land Base

4,416

National Forest Lands
Currently Available
for Timber Harvest

Available Lands
in Other Ownerships

Unprogrammed Lands —
not suitable or
otherwise not
organized for timber
production; these
include unregulated
and some of the
marginal lands.

Deferred Lands —
not in the
current timber base,
pending wilderness
decisions

Sources:
  1) State of Washington,
Department of Natural
Resources, Washington
Forest Productivity Study,
Phase III, Part II, January
1982.
  2) U.S. Department of
Agriculture, Forest Ser-
vice, RARE II data and
Timber Management Plans.

TABLE 2

The Effect of Wilderness Designation on Annual Harvest Volume in Washington State

A board foot is a volume of
wood 12 inches long
by 12 inches wide by
1 inch thick.

Potential Annual Harvest Volume
in Wilderness Proposal

National Forest
Allowable Cut 1980

Maximum
Impact of
Wilderness
Designation
on Statewide
Harvest Volume
= 3.0%

1,500

Average Annual Statewide Harvest, 1970-1980

208

112

1,000   2,000   3,000   4,000   5,432   6,717

Millions of Board Feet

National forest
allowable cut
(volume prepared for sale)

Average volume from
other ownerships, 1970-1980

Deferred lands, not in the current
timber base, pending wilderness decisions and
other forest lands not organized
or programmed for harvest —
the unregulated and some of
the marginal lands.

Sources:
  1) State of Washington,
Department of Natural
Resources, Timber Harvest
Reports and Washington
Mill Surveys.
  2) U.S. Department of
Agriculture, Forest Ser-
vice, RARE II data,
Timber Management Plans,
and Production, Prices,
Employment, and Trade
in Northwest Forest
Industries.